TEEN-AGERS ASK MORE QUESTIONS

Books by Sheila John Daly

Blondes Prefer Gentlemen
Party Fun
Personality Plus!
Pretty, Please
Questions Teen-Agers Ask
Teen-Agers Ask More Questions

Teen-Agers

Ask More

~ Questions

Answered by SHEILA JOHN DALY

ILLUSTRATED BY BOB KELLY

DODD, MEAD & COMPANY, NEW YORK

*For Doc
and
for Peter
again and always*

Introduction

Being a teen-ager is fascinating, fun—and sometimes frustrating. You're meeting countless problems and challenges, many of them for the first time in your young life. And you're looking for answers.

In the past eighteen years, as a syndicated newspaper columnist for teens, I've received tens of thousands of letters from teen-agers, asking for advice, help and information. This book is a cross-section of the questions that have been asked most often—and the answers to them. Knowing the answers to the problems that trouble you (and to many questions you haven't yet asked) makes the exciting, but sometimes difficult, business of growing up easier and more satisfying.

Here, as in *Questions Teen-Agers Ask*, you will find something of your life, your friends, your family, your worries and pleasures and dreams. Hopefully, this book may help you to find more fun and happiness in your teen-aged life.

SHEILA JOHN DALY

Contents

1 : *Every-Date Manners*

Boy-Girl Etiquette

Q. *The fellow I'm dating has asked me for a picture of myself for his room. This poses a problem. The best picture I've ever had taken is one that an amateur photograhper I used to date shot of me. He gave me several copies and I'd like to give one to my new beau. But what will he think if he finds out who was behind the camera?*

A. He'll think, "What a good picture of Sue!" and "Aren't I lucky to have it!" Tell him, if it will keep your conscience clear, that an old friend who is a shutterbug snapped it — and let it go at that.

Q. *My girl friend has asked me to arrange a blind date for one of her gal pals. I've lined up a buddy who's willing to take the girl out sight unseen. Should I just send him to pick his date up on the night (we're doubling), or how should it be handled?*

A. The first few minutes of a blind date are the roughest. The best idea is for you and your girl to pick up your buddy and go together to pick up his date. Then you can perform the introductions and help get the conversation rolling. You'll all have a better time if you're around to help break the ice at the start.

Q. *About two weeks ago my buddy asked me to go on a blind date with his girl's cousin, who had just moved to town. I'm leery of blind dates and, besides, I was broke, so I told him "No." He asked me to take the girl as a special favor to him. (It was for a big dance and his frill said she couldn't go unless her cousin came, too.) He offered to give me the money for the evening's expenses. I finally agreed and, big surprise, had a marvelous time. The girl turned out to be great, and I want to continue dating her. But I'm afraid she'll find out that I was practically paid to take her out the first time.*

A. No need to nurse a guilty conscience just because the other fellow picked up the tab for the first evening's fun. You *were* broke, you *did* do him a favor, and how did you know the plot would have such a happy ending! If it will make you feel better, tell your buddy you consider his financing the first date a loan, repay him, and begin dating the girl with a clear conscience and an empty wallet—with her picture in it!

Q. *The boys I go out with seem to think it's square to be courteous. They're nice fellows, from good families, but it never seems to occur to them to hold a door open for a girl, help her with her coat or hold her chair. My father is a gentleman of the old school, and I'm used to courtly behavior from men. It bothers me to have the boys I date so rough and tumble.*

A. A girl can tame a wild man, but it takes time and patience. First of all, you have to *look* feminine and *act* feminine. If a boy is used to seeing you toting books or wielding a field hockey stick, he has to adjust his thinking to your date-time personality. It helps if you hang back a little when approaching doors, to remind him gently that he's the male. Hand him your coat when you want help with it, hesitate beside your chair to give him a chance to whip it out with a flourish. But never delay so long that you pointedly call attention to his etiquette lapses and make him feel self-conscious. And be sure you don't go too far with the fragile flower act; it's too short a step to wallflower.

Q. *The boy I date won't come up to my apartment to pick pick me up for the evening. He says it's too hard to find a parking place in our crowded area (mostly apartment buildings, where street space is at a premium) and he wants me to be waiting in the lobby of our building. My parents disapprove of this and I find it unflattering that he isn't willing to go to the extra trouble.*

A. Time for a friendly ultimatum. Let your fellow friend know that a date includes pick up and delivery, even if it's inconvenient for him to be gallant.

Q. *I met a girl at a dance given by a youth club I belong to. I walked her home that night and asked her for a date, but she says she can't go out with "pickups." I think she likes me, though. Any suggestions?*

A. Have the director of the youth club or one of the dance chaperones make a formal introduction, then ask the girl if you may come over to visit some evening. Once you've won the nod of approval from her parents, you'll no longer be considered a "pickup."

Q. *I have a small but important question. Most of the kids in my class stop off at a certain drugstore after classes for a snack. Usually I go with my best friend, but fellows often come and sit with us in our booth. Who should pick up the checks?*

A. After-school snacks are strictly Dutch treat, unless a boy specifically invites you to join him. Otherwise, the boys wouldn't have any jingling money left over for taking you out on after-dark dates, and *then* wouldn't you set up a wail!

Q. *For the past three months I've been dating a boy who has made me understand the expression "painfully polite." He's so courteous he's driving me wild! He's not really stuffy, but he gives that impression, because he jumps up whenever a female comes into the room (even my eleven-year-old sister), and is so busy making sure he doesn't miss opening a door or holding a chair that I have the feeling he isn't paying attention to the conversation. I've griped about boys being oafish and inattentive before, but I think this Dresden-doll treatment is worse. How can I make the boy realize that I won't break in a million pieces if he forgets to hold my chair or help me with my coat?*

A. Ideally, good manners should come so naturally that they're not noticed. But this takes practice—and that's what your fellow friend is doing. Within a few months (or a few years) all these small attentions he pays to females will become second nature to him and won't seem so obvious. Meanwhile, *you* relax and enjoy the situation. You never had it so good—and may never again!

Q. *I'm going with a girl who must eat vitamin pills like peanuts. Along about midnight I'm ready to call it an evening, but she's just getting her second wind. When I'm ready to take her home, she wants to listen to another set at the jazz joint or stop at a coffeehouse for espresso or go for a moonlight ride. I can't keep my eyelids propped open on dates or in class the next day, but I hate to fade out on her.*

A. Don't let your high-spirited girl turn you into a Don Wan. Make it clear that when the clock strikes midnight, the bell tolls for you. A date isn't much fun when one of the partners is blurry and bleary-eyed, so escort her home when *you* feel like it. But before you tell her good night, ask her what brand of vitamins she takes!

Q. *There's one boy in our crowd, two years older than the rest of us, who has been away to college and who always acts like a real big deal. Whenever he sees one of us girls, he gives her a big hug and a kiss on the cheek, and then stands with his arm around her shoulder, while he talks to her. I think he's being fresh while pretending not to be, and I don't like it.*

A. If Big Boy doesn't take the hint when you slip out from his embrace, just tell him straightforwardly that you don't like to be hugged or kissed in such a casual fashion. Such sticky problems can be solved by a few direct words of basic English.

Q. *When introducing teen-agers to each other, is it really necessary to say, "Miss Sally Jones, may I present Mr. John Jenkins?" That's what all the etiquette books I've read say, but it seems awfully formal to me.*

A. If you used such an introduction technique, your friends would glance down to see if you were still wearing high-button shoes. Life is more informal these days, and teen-agers are apt to start off friendships on a first-name basis. But males are still presented to females, in the old tradition. Being a girl still rates *some* privileges!

Q. *The boy I date uses bad language frequently, and this embarrasses me. I think he does it just to shock me. I don't know how to get him to stop. He's a nice boy in every other way.*

A. Tell the boy you're red-faced with embarrassment every time he turns the air blue with unattractive words. Make it clear that either he stops—or you stop dating him. Bet he makes the right choice between foul mouth and fair maiden!

Q. *A boy I go with and I disagree on politics. Our arguments are pretty noisy whenever the subject comes up. We both feel rather deeply, and harsh words get exchanged. There's a city election coming up and I'm afraid we'll scarcely be speaking to each other most of the time.*

A. Most people find it impossible to debate politics calmly. It looks as if you'll have to decide whether your romance or the expression of your political convictions is more important to you. If you and your guy are going to spend every date night debating issues, you'll end up being terribly well-informed enemies. It's probably a good idea to declare a moratorium on political discussions until after the election, if you want your romance to survive. Decide whether you can keep your mouth shut and a smile on your face simultaneously.

Q. *My boy friend and I disagree on a point of etiquette and hope you can help us. He maintains that it's bad manners to put on lipstick at the table after a meal, but I have seen dozens of well-dressed, well-mannered women do this. I know you shouldn't powder your nose or comb your hair publicly, but I can't see anything wrong with a quick, discreet application of lipstick to repair the damage done by food and drink. What do you think?*

A. You're not going to be drummed out of polite society just because you freshen your lipstick at the table, but some males find the practice offensive. They like to believe that good looks are a magic done with mirrors. And those mirrors are in the ladies' room!

Q. *A girl from our class is working as an apprentice at the local summer theater, and she has a walk-on part in next week's show. A group of us fellows are planning to go see her, and we would like to go backstage afterward. But we're wondering if she would consider that cornball and "nonprofessional."*

A. Your gal pal will be flattered if you come backstage to visit her after the show, and devastated if you don't. The only thing that could make her debut even more complete would be for you all to ask her, semi-seriously, to autograph your programs.

Q. *You'd think it was impossible for a guy to reach my age (sixteen) without knowing how to ask a girl to dance. But it's true; I don't. I guess socially I'm a schnook, but I panic every time I'm ready to ask a girl to take a turn around the floor. I'm too embarrassed to ask the guys what they say, and my mother's suggestion ("May I have the pleasure*

*of the next dance?") sounds too square. I don't want to
spend the rest of my nights in the stag line.*

A. If you walked up to a girl at a dance today and said,
"May I have the pleasure of the next dance?" she'd expect
you to be a whiz at the minuet. That approach is too formal
for today's relaxed living. But there's nothing wrong with a
simple, straightforward question like "Would you like to
dance?" Then hope you get an equally simple, straightforward answer like *"Yes!"*

Q. *A girl I like accepted a bid to a big dance from me
three months ago. Yesterday, she came down with appendi-
citis. The dance is two days away, and I'd still like to go. Do
you think it's too late to invite someone else? Most of the
crowd knows I invited the girl, but I have the tickets and the
dinner jacket and the flowers ordered. Would another girl
be insulted at being a last-minute choice?*

A. Your girl probably feels badly about leaving you in
the lurch. Why not ask her if she'd like to send in a substitute? Undoubtedly there are at least two or three eager
females who'd welcome a bid, however eleventh-hour. You
may get stuck with an also-ran type, but at least you'll
get to the dance.

Q. *Maybe you'll think I'm a nut for not knowing the
answer to this question at seventeen, but my family has
just moved to a large city from a small town and for the
first time I'm dating girls who live in apartment houses. Is
a guy supposed to take his date to the door of her apartment,
or drop her at the elevator? And if he drops her at the
elevator, when does he get a chance to kiss her good night?*

A. If the elevator is self-service, the gentlemanly thing to do is deliver the girl safely to her apartment door. Otherwise, you can leave that chore to the elevator man, if you prefer. But even if it's an attended elevator, there's no rule that says you can't go along for the ride, and the good night kiss, when you're so inclined. Your girl would probably be disappointed if you didn't—if she is so inclined, too. Better make sure of this!

Q. *My boy friend is pretty polite, but he insists on honking his horn when he picks me up for a date, instead of coming to the door. I can't stand this, but I'm afraid I'll lose him if I demand door-to-door delivery on dates.*

A. Don't *demand* courtesy from your date, just act as if you *expect* it! Next time he honks his horn, bide your time. Eventually, he'll come to the door like a gentleman, and you can pretend that's what you expected him to do all along.

Q. *I've just started dating, and I find all sorts of etiquette confusing. For instance, who goes first down the aisle of a movie theater? And who goes first to a table in a restaurant? And who gives the order to the waiter?*

A. If there's an usher handy, the girl follows him down the theater aisle, and her date brings up the rear, Indian fashion. But if no usher is on hand, the boy goes first, groping through the dusky light to find two on the aisle. In both cases, the girl goes first into the seats, murmuring apologies to anyone whose feet she's stepping over. In a restaurant, once the boy has asked the headwaiter or hostess for a table, the girl goes first to the table after the headwaiter or hostess, and waits for her date to pull out her chair and seat her. Then she gives her food order to her date (asking him first what he recommends, to get an idea of the price range he can afford), who passes it on to the waiter.

Q. *What do I owe to a girl who invited me to a turnabout dance and provided the tickets? I'd never taken her out before, though I know her from school. We had a pretty good time and I'd like to do the right thing.*

A. You owe the girl at least one return engagement. And you may be surprised to discover that the second evening will be more fun. When a girl invites a boy out for a turnabout date, she's likely to feel nervous and unsure of herself. But bolstered by the knowledge that you like her well enough to ask her out yourself, she may blossom on that second date.

Q. *When a guy has to park the car in a lot or garage on a date night, should his girl come with him or should she be dropped off at the party or theater or whatever?*

A. If you're just a twosome, the girl would probably prefer riding to the parking lot with you, rather than being left to wait alone in front of the theater or party place, unless the weather is bad. But if you're behind the wheel on a double date, it's better manners (and less clutter in the parking lot) to drop off your date and the other couple and be car jockey on your own. The same rules apply when it's pickup time.

Q. *I'm seventeen but have never gotten over being rather shy around girls. I've managed to hold hands with several and kiss a few I really cared about, but I'm still kind of awkward with females. One thing that really bugs me is to dance with a girl in a bareback dress. I just don't know where to put my hand; to me it seems very intimate to have my hand on her bare back. But I'm not so cornball I'd put my handkerchief between my hand and her epidermis. Any ideas?*

A. Just zero in on that area when fabric meets skin. You can still maintain a graceful dancing stance if your hand is just above her waist. If her dress is cut any lower than that, better take the girl home—before the police do!

Q. *I'm as polite as the next fellow, but I think my girl is too demanding. The other night it was snowing when we came out of the movie and I went to get the car so she wouldn't get her little tootsies wet. When I pulled up in front of the theater, she waited till I climbed out and walked around to open the car door for her. I almost started a traffic jam, with horns honking furiously and cars backed up while I played the white knight. Why couldn't she have opened the door and hopped in like a big, strong, healthy girl, which she is?*

A. It would have been adequate if you'd leaned over and opened the door for your date from the driver's seat—and much safer. If this sensible shortcut makes her sit and sulk, let her sit and sulk—at home.

Q. *The boy I date thinks he is a real comedian, and he is pretty fast and funny with the cracks. The place he shines, though, is at the movies, when he keeps up a running commentary on the film, the acting, the romantic technique of the leading man, etc. I admit I'm amused, but I'm also mortified. He annoys people sitting near us, and last week-*

end the usher finally asked us to leave. I don't want to step
all over his lines, but I'd much rather he behaved less like a
nut. How can I get my message across?

A. Try English. As long as you keep giggling at his antics
and he doesn't sense your disapproval, your date will play
each occasion for laughs. Let him know that, unless he lets
the performers handle the patter, you're going to walk out
on his one-man show—and on him. A comic can't stand to
lose his audience, so he'll probably reschedule his act for
after the movie.

Q. *There's a roughneck bunch of boys in our school who*
get their kicks from making rude or lewd remarks at girls on
the street. I never know how to act when I have to pass
them. How can I put them in their place?

A. Treat them as you would any other annoying minor
pesky problem: ignore them and hope they'll go away. Any
reply, any criticism, will only egg them on. So keep your
eyes straight ahead, look as if you're a gal in a hurry, on the
way to do something important, and simply pretend they
don't exist. For you, they don't.

Q. *An historical movie is coming to the neighborhood*
theater next week and our teacher suggested that we all go
to see it. Practically the whole class is planning to meet in
front of the theater on Saturday afternoon to see it together.
Should the boys buy the girls' tickets? Most of us are sort
of paired off, even though we're not going steady.

A. This is strictly Dutch treat. Step right up to the box
office with your money in your hot little hand. Boys have a
hard enough time paying for the dates they themselves

arrange. Don't expect them to pick up the tab when the teacher is making the plans!

Presents and Posies

Q. I was hoping that my boy friend would give me a gold charm for my charm bracelet for my birthday. I certainly dropped enough hints. Instead, he gave me a heart-shaped locket on a chain. I think lockets are corny, and I haven't worn it. His feelings are hurt, but I'm disappointed, too.

A. Sounds as if you're short on charm, as well as charms. A carefully chosen present rates a big smile and an enthusiastic thank you, not the sulks. If you cannot be gracious and grateful enough to wear the gold heart around your neck, have it put on your bracelet. The boy's wearing his heart on his sleeve; the least you can do is to wear his heart on your wrist.

Q. There's a girl at school I've never dated, though we've worked together on a couple of committees and I think she knows I go for her. Now her birthday is coming and I'd like to send her a double-whammy present, so that when I finally work up the nerve to ask her out, she just won't be able to say "No." Any great ideas?

A. Try to think of a smallish present that would intrigue her, arouse her curiosity. Sending a red rose a day for a week and then a dozen is an old technique, slightly corny, but irresistible to sentimental females. Or check with one of her close friends to find out what the gal's secret heart is yearning for, and buy it. (Mink coats and Thunderbirds excepted, of course!) You might send her a scrapbook stamped with her initials and the first pages filled with clippings about her from the school and local paper. Or really play it cool and send her an ID bracelet with your picture in it and a note saying, "In six months, I'll ask you to wear this." That ought to rouse her curiosity enough to accept the first date.

Q. *I'm a seventeen-year-old boy and have been going steady with Janie for almost a year. When I was shopping for her Christmas present, I saw a great looking nightgown in a store window and ordered it. My mother flipped when it was delivered and says I* can't *give it to Janie. Is she right, or is she just being a stuffy mother?*

A. Even if you were engaged to Janie, a nightgown would be considered too intimate a present, so race right back to the department store to exchange it for a more appropriate gift—or ask your mother to do it for you, if you'd find the chore too embarrassing. You might also ask your mother to help you pick out a proper present. She knows something about female taste—and about etiquette!

Q. *I'm a sixteen-year-old guy who doesn't really know very much about girls or dating. I've asked a girl to a formal dance at school next week, and I don't know what to do about a corsage. I have a feeling I goofed when I brought flowers to the same girl for a Christmas dance. She didn't say anything, but there was a definite lack of enthusiasm when she opened the florist box and found sweetheart roses.*

A. Check with the girl's mother to find out what color dress your date is wearing, and then take your problem to a friendly florist. Things to remember: girls usually prefer smallish corsages, which don't interfere with the lines of their dresses and can be worn, if necessary, pinned to the

evening bag or tied to the wrist. You can't go wrong with a single gardenia or camellia or, if you're flush, an orchid. But go easy on the ribbons and ferns and greenery. The flowers shouldn't be lost among the trimmings, and neither should the girl!

Q. *A girl in our class is having a birthday party next week and I'm invited. I was planning to buy her some perfume or a book or something, but yesterday she came up to me and said, "If you're wondering what I'd like for my birthday, there's a bracelet in the jewelry store on Fourth Street . . ." and then she described, in detail, what she wanted. I looked at the bracelet after school, and it's way out of my price range. I got angry. Isn't it terrible manners to be so specific about what you hope to get as a present? I may not go to her darn party at all.*

A. Sounds as if your gal pal has confused a guest list with a shopping list. Of course, her asking outright for a certain present is very poor manners. You can give her a subtle lesson in etiquette by ignoring her request entirely and giving her whatever gift you choose. She may be miffed and cross you off her invitation list for next year, but that's not much of a loss.

Q. *For a big dance, my boy friend sent me a really junky corsage, huge and ugly and loaded with sparkle-covered ribbon. I just couldn't wear it and pretended I'd forgotten to bring it. He hasn't spoken to me since the night of the dance.*

A. In choosing an unattractive corsage, your fellow showed bad judgment. In refusing to wear it, you showed bad manners. You should have pinned the flowers to your evening bag and saved his pride—and the romance.

Q. *Our prom is next week and I'm going with the same fellow who took me to a formal dance during Christmas vacation. He's wonderful, but he doesn't seem to have any taste in flowers. Last time he sent me a ghastly, though expensive, corsage. It was so heavy I had to pin it on my evening bag, but it still looked terrible. How can I drop a hint so I'll get something decent this time?*

A. On your next stroll, steer your fellow past a florist shop and linger in front of the window. Show him the gardenias or camellias or tiny orchids and sigh wistfully, "I guess that's just about my favorite flower." It he doesn't get your message, better put in for a brighter date mate.

Q. *My parents gave me a sweet sixteen party two nights ago. Everyone brought me wonderful presents, and I said enthusiastic thanks when I opened each one. Do I still have to write thank-you letters? My mother says "Yes," but I think it's unnecessary.*

A. It isn't really necessary to add written thanks to the oh's and ah's you expressed as you tore off the wrapping paper. But you'll tag yourself as an extra-thoughtful person if you take a few moments to dash off a note to everyone who spent time and money choosing something to say "Happy brithday!" It's a gracious thing to do and, to be practical, they'll remember you more fondly when your seventeenth birthday comes around!

Q. *Recently I had a big birthday party and there were so many presents that I didn't open them during the festivities. When it came time to unwrap them, I found two gifts without cards. By a process of elimination, I know these gifts came from two fellows I've dated, but I don't know which one brought which. Should I just send a general thank-you note ("Thank you for the lovely present" sort or thing) or should I try to find out which is whose?*

A. Here's a perfectly good excuse to make telephone calls to two attractive males. Don't pass up a golden chance like that! Phone both fellows, explain what happened and ask which present each sent. Then you can make your thank yous prettily—and explicitly. When a boy has spent time and cash picking out the right gift, he wants to be sure you know *he* sent it.

Q. *I want to buy my steady girl an ankle bracelet for her birthday. She has beautiful legs, and I think an ankle brace-let would help call attention to her slim ankles. My mother says that such jewelry is "cheap." What is your opinion?*

A. Taste is a matter of taste, and it's hard to say whether an ankle bracelet is "cheap" jewelry. But why not accept your mother's judgement that the choice just isn't right for your girl? She's a woman and probably knows more about female tastes. Ask her for other suggestions or listen around for hints dropped by your girl, then decide on something else.

Q. *I'm fifteen and go with a boy the same age who is just beginning to get some fuzz on his chin. I think it's time he began to shave, and I'd like to give him an electric razor for his birthday next month. What do you think of the idea?*

A. Fathers are usually in charge of that department. An electric razor, especially his first, is too personal a gift to give a fellow—and too expensive. Appeal to his male vanity by giving him after-shave lotion instead. He'll get the message, but not in such personal terms.

Q. *My boy friend gave me a bikini bathing suit for my birthday last week and keeps nagging me to wear it. I'd be embarrassed to be seen in it, it's so skimpy—and I don't think he should have given me such a personal gift anyway. How can I tell him?*

A. You should have explained to the boy that you couldn't accept his present as soon as you received it. You'll still have to do so, even though he won't be able to return it to the store (most stores won't allow bathing suits to be exchanged). He has learned an expensive lesson in gift-giving, but, at least, it's one he'll remember, with pain in his wallet.

Q. *I gave a girl a bracelet for a birthday present over a month ago and I've never seen her wear it. Do you think she doesn't like it? If she doesn't, I'd like to return it and let her pick out something she likes better.*

A. Why not make the offer to the girl? Either she'll accept and end up with a piece of jewelry she really likes, or she'll realize your feelings are hurt by her indifference to your present and begin wearing it occasionally. Stir up the situation a bit with your offer to exchange the gift. *Something* will happen.

Q. *For my birthday, a boy I've dated for months gave me an inexpensive key ring. I'm annoyed and hurt, partly because I've presented him with expensive gifts in the past, partly because he has a huge allowance. I'm not gold-digging. I just find it insulting and bad manners to be brushed off so cheaply. He knows better. He pretends he loves me, but certainly doesn't show it.*

A. Tell the boy, quite calmly, that you're hurt, and explain why. You'll either antagonize him sufficiently to be crossed off his date list, or shame him into shopping more thoughtfully and realistically next time a big occasion comes up.

Q. *Is a sweater too personal a gift to give my girl for her birthday? My mother knits great-looking bulky ski sweaters and she's offered to make one for my best girl. But she's wondering if it's in good taste.*

A. A homemade sweater is in perfectly good taste for your girl's birthday, especially one your mother has knitted, and the extra thoughtfulness that went into it will make her feel warm all over!

Q. *I've always heard that a guy should ask what color dress a girl is wearing to a dance, so that he can pick the right flowers. What's a fellow supposed to do when he asked his girl and she said her dress is "sort of* orchid-colored"?

A. Give in gracefully! An orchid is part of the prom dream of many girls, so dig deep into your jeans and come up with the price of that posy, if at all possible. Your girl wasn't very subtle, but girls seldom are about something they want badly. She'll love you for pleasing her and making the big night perfect.

Q. *What does a girl do with an expensive portable radio received for Christmas from a boy she's never even dated? On Christmas Eve a beautifully wrapped package was delivered, from a boy who has invited me out several times. I've always turned him down because I just don't like him. I guess he thought this grand gesture would make me change my mind. I realize it should be returned, but how? I don't even know his phone number.*

A. Certainly someone you know knows the boy's address. Best method of returning the present is to wrap it carefully and send it to him through the mail, with a note saying you're flattered by his interest but you can't possibly accept the gift. This was probably his last all-out effort to gain your attention. He gets A for effort, if not for good taste.

Q. *I've been dating a fellow for about six weeks, and I'm not sure if he plans to give me a Christmas present. I'd like to give him a gift, but I don't want to embarrass him—or myself—by giving him a present and then finding out he has nothing for me. We have a date on Christmas night.*

A. Your fellow friend probably isn't going to show up empty-handed on Christmas night, so it's fairly safe to buy him a present. Choose something not too expensive, not too personal—and returnable. Have it all wrapped and tied prettily, but be sure to hold onto the sales check! There's a small chance you'll have to trek back to the store after the holiday and return the merchandise, but it's a very small chance, and one worth taking.

Q. *My girl friend gave me a sweater for my birthday, and my mother thinks it's too personal a gift for me to accept. My mother doesn't know that we've been going steady for almost five months (my folks wouldn't approve, so I can't tell my mother) and that the girl knit the sweater herself. If I return it, my girl will die of hurt feelings. And if I keep it, my mother won't speak to me.*

A. Find your mother in a calm moment and tell her the truth. She'll be annoyed at your clandestine romance (as she should be; it's never a good idea to try to keep secrets that break family rules) and she may insist that you put the twosome on a more casual basis. Perhaps she'll understand what time and affection went into your gift, and relent enough to let you keep it. But you'll have to take her into your confidence first. You should make the situation very clear to your girl friend, too. She may not be aware that you have been hiding things from your parents or how they feel about going steady.

Q. *I'd been going with a boy for two months before Christmas and, of course, he gave me a present. Two days later, we had a huge argument, which I honestly think was his fault. I have two questions. Do I have to return his present? And do I have an obligation to go on dating him if I don't? During the fight, I saw a side of him I never knew before, and I honestly don't want to go out with him again.*

A. The fellow didn't "buy" you with his Christmas gift, so you needn't feel obligated to keep on going out with him, now that the glow is gone. Returning his present is a dramatic, but futile, gesture. Just let the romance die quietly, with no bitterness, no recriminations, and no deluge of returned love letters, photographs or presents.

Q. *I really slaved to earn my letter in football this season and I'm proud to wear my letter sweater. The other night my date complained that she was cold and I let her borrow my sweater, expecting her to return it when I took her home. She didn't say a word about it, and I was too surprised to ask for it. The next day she wore it to school and everybody thinks we're going steady.*

A. Call her tonight and tell her you'd like to stop over and pick up your sweater. Don't take no for an answer. You earned your letter. She didn't.

Q. *A boy I've been dating gave me a portable radio for my birthday. Because I knew my parents would set up a howl about my accepting such an expensive gift, I kept it a secret. It wasn't that I wanted the radio so desperately, but the boy was excited about giving it to me and I didn't want to hurt his feelings. Now my mother found out about the radio and knows the whole story. She insists I return it, though I've had it for three weeks. What can I do?*

A. There's nothing to do but return the radio, along with a polite and apologetic explanation of your reasons. It would have been less awkward to do this as soon as you received the gift—which is just another way of saying that honesty *is* the best—and easiest—policy!

Q. *On Christmas Eve my steady came to take me to midnight services and brought me my present, which I opened on the spot. I'd been looking forward to a bracelet (he'd been hinting that was what he planned to give me) and when I opened the package and found a compact, my disappointment really showed. In fact, I burst into tears! I was overtired from the holiday rush and just couldn't help myself, though I knew it was selfish of me, and I tried hard to fight back the tears. His feelings were hurt, of course, and he went home. I'm just miserable and don't know how he'll ever forgive me—or how I can forgive myself.*

A. Emotions often run high around the holidays, when everyone is both tired and keyed-up. Now that the boy is over his own disappointment at your reaction he probably realizes this. Phone him or drop him a note, apologizing for the scene. Thank him for the compact. Tell him how much you really love it, and invite him to drop over. He'll probably be willing to forgive and forget if you make the first move.

Q. *I gave a girl I'd been dating ever since Thanksgiving a present for Christmas, but she didn't give me anything. Now I feel like a fool. Was I rushing things, since we'd been going together for only a month? And should my feelings be hurt that she didn't think enough of me to give me a present?*

A. No need to nurse hurt feelings. With only a month's date life behind you, the girl couldn't have been sure you planned to give her a Christmas present, and both you and she would have been red-faced if she'd played Santa, and you hadn't. But it was perfectly fine for you to give her a remembrance. It's still a man's world, and you're supposed to be the aggressor!

Q. *I just heard that my boy friend plans to give me a puppy for my birthday. He's all excited at the idea and couldn't help telling his buddy, who told me. Frankly, I dislike dogs, don't want one and am quite sure we wouldn't be allowed to keep one in our apartment. What am I going to do?*

A. Send word back through your beau boy's buddy that there's a big NO DOGS ALLOWED rule in your apartment building, and then hope hard that he hasn't already invested all his cash in an appealing small pup. They're not returnable, like gloves, for a different size and color!

Q. *For my birthday my boy friend gave me a very nice piece of costume jewelry, and I really do love it. But I don't want to wear it all the time. It doesn't go with everything, and I get tired of it. But he acts hurt if I go out with him and don't wear the pin. Isn't there some sort of compromise?*

A. Tell your beau boy the truth, that the pin is a favorite with you, but it doesn't go with your entire wardrobe. Whenever possible, wear it on date nights, but don't feel apologetic if you don't. He just wants to be reassured that you like him and think his taste is good. Bolster his ego in varied ways so that whether or not you wear his gift is no longer so important to him.

Q. *When my best girl graduates, I can afford to give her only one gift. I know she's dying to have an orchid to wear to the party after the ceremonies. I'd prefer to give her something lasting like a pen or bracelet or compact, but I don't want to disappoint her.*

A. If your girl's graduation night isn't going to be complete without an orchid, then send her one. To a sentimental girl, pleasant memories of a perfect evening and the corsage ribbon pressed in her yearbook are as lasting as something solid silver.

Q. *Ever since I was a Brownie Scout, I've loved to work in crafts. For several years I've been making homemade birthday and Christmas presents: wastebaskets decorated with maps or newspaper clippings or hobby motifs, address books covered with pretty fabrics, prints of modern painters which I frame myself, etc. I've always though people enjoyed these gifts, but one of my friends says it's insulting and cheap to give do-it-yourself presents. Is she right?*

A. Your "friend" couldn't be more wrong. One of the most flattering presents to give anyone is something you cared enough to make yourself. So go right ahead and turn out special handmades for everyone on your Christmas list—

except that mercenary creature who criticized. She doesn't deserve such personalized attention.

Entertaining Etiquette

Q. *My girl's parents belong to the local country club, and I'm often invited there as their guest, to swim or play tennis or to parties. It's the sort of entertainment I can't possibly hope to repay. I'm beginning to feel funny about accepting their hospitality so frequently. And yet it doesn't seem fair to expect my girl to swim with me at the public beach just because I've got a bad case of pride.*

A. Many families use a country club as a "home away from home" for summer entertainment, and you should be no more leery of accepting these invitations than you would bids to attend at-home parties. Relax and enjoy the summer; sounds as if you never had it so good. Just be sure to initiate and finance enough dates so you don't feel like a gigolo.

Q. *When a guy goes to a party given by a girl, does he thank her or her mother at the end of the evening? I'm never quite sure what is expected.*

A. Your thanks should go both to the girl hostess and her mother. If her mother isn't nearby when you're saying good night (she's probably busy in the kitchen washing glasses!), then at least be sure to say to the girl, "Please tell your mother thank you for me, too. I've had a wonderful time."

Q. *I went to a party the other night and in some rough-housing two long-play records belonging to the host were broken. Some of the guests think we should divvy up the expense of replacing them; others think broken records are just one of the hazards of party-giving.*

A. It should be a fairly painless process to split the expense of replacing the records, and it will assure you all of being invited back again.

Q. *One of my best friends has borrowed her aunt's lake-front cottage for a week-long house party, and I've been invited. It's to be for eight girls and should be lots of fun, but I've just discovered that they don't plan to have anyone older around as a chaperone. Most of the girls think that our age (seventeen) is old enough to be responsible for ourselves. It's true that it's an all-female group, but the guys will be coming out for parties, and I'm just afraid things will get out of hand, or at least look bad, if there isn't an adult present. I hate to say no to the plans. My parents say they'll trust my judgment, though they don't approve of the no-chaperone deal.*

A. If you can't stir up a little enthusiasm among the rest of the girls for the idea of a chaperone, then better plan to stay home. House-party fun wouldn't be dampened by the presence of a couple in their late twenties (or a pair of older girls or an aunt or mother) and you'd all feel more comfortable and "respectable." Check with two or three of the other house party guests, and we'll bet you'll find them as apprehensive about the plans as you are. Among you, you may be able to persuade the hostess to include a chaperone or two on the guest list.

Q. *I'm going to spend a week with a girl from my dorm at school. She comes from a wealthy family, with two servants, and I'm not quite sure how to behave. For instance, do I make my own bed and do my own laundry, or what?*

A. No matter how many servants in the house, it's still

good manners to make your bed and keep your own guest quarters neat, with clothes put away and towels hung up. You can plan to pack enough "outside" clothes to see you through the week, and do your own minor personal laundry, hosiery and lingerie. If your hostess thinks you're overworking, she'll let you know fast enough, and you can take the cue from her.

Q. *Please help me out of my dilemma. I'm seventeen and have been dating a boy nineteen. He invited me up to spend the weekend at his folks' summer cottage. I'd love to go (I know his parents quite well and get along with them) but to tell the truth, I can't help suspecting males of being predatory. For instance, I have a sneaking suspicion that I might get there and discover his parents were away for the weekend or something. How can I be sure his invitation is on the up and up?*

A. To make it official, the weekend invitation should be echoed by the boy's mother, your hostess. Tell the boy you'd enjoy spending the weekend with his family and if he'll have his mother write to invite you, you'll dash off an acceptance in a hurry. Simple as that!

Q. *I've invited my girl up to my family's summer place for the weekend. I've never had a girl guest before (I'm sixteen) and I don't know if I'm supposed to send her her railroad tickets, or if she's expected to pay her own way. It's only a matter of five dollars or so round trip, but I want to do the right thing.*

A. It's up to you to provide the girl with entertainment when she's your guest, but the railroad tickets and the hostess present to your mother come out of the gal's piggy bank. Girls have very little social expense, so be grateful for this one time when she has to pick up the tab for *something*.

Q. *I went to a party given by a girl friend the other night. When I got there, I discovered that her parents had gone to a movie, and there were no adults in the house, just eight teen-age couples. My mother has always insisted that parties I attend be chaperoned. I told my date I'd have to leave, and we went to a movie instead. My boy friend thinks I'm sort of kooky and my girl friend is furious at me for not staying at her shindig. Did I do right?*

A. Yes, you did right. Let's hope your friends who remained at the unchaperoned party can say the same thing!

Q. *About three weeks ago, I was invited to have Sunday dinner with my boy friend and his family. They were very friendly and his mother made a delicious dinner. Afterward, we all sat chatting in the living room until it was time for me to go home. He's been complaining ever since that I embarrassed him by not offering to help with the dishes. I thought it would spoil the nice effect of the company dinner if we all trooped out to the kitchen and plunged into hot, soapy water. Who was right?*

A. You were. You appreciated the party and showed good judgment by keeping a party mood. Don't dream too bright dreams of the future with this fellow. He sounds as if he may put you on a pedestal just high enough to reach the dishpan!

2 : *Every-Day Manners*

Letter Perfect

Q. *I never got around to writing thank-you notes for all my Christmas presents. The holiday parties were hectic and I had a lot of work to do when I got back to school. I'm hoping everyone will think my letters got lost in the mail, because a month after Christmas is too late to write. But my mother keeps nagging me and saying "better late than never!"*

A. Most people would rather have an enthusiastic thank-you note ("I've been so busy listening to my new dance record I've hardly had time for anything else—like writing to tell you how much I thank you for it.") late than not at all. Your mother is right. Whip off those letters, or people won't be so eager to remember you next holiday season.

Q. *A girl I know from school is on an auto trip with her parents and is bombarding me with post cards. I never dated her, and I don't understand this sudden interest in me. Do you think she expects me to take her out when she gets home?*

A. Obviously the girl is *hoping* you'll be interested enough to ask her for a date. But even a telegram a day wouldn't obligate you to ask her out if you didn't want to.

Q. *During spring vacation, when I was home from prep school, I met a girl and took her out quite a few times. She seemed to like me as much as I liked her, and promised to write to me when I returned to school. Two weeks have passed and I still haven't heard from her. Should I just forget about her, since she didn't keep her promise?*

A. The girl promised to write, but she certainly expected you'd be the first to use Uncle Sam as a middle man. Dash off a fast letter to her, telling her how much fun you had over the vacation and how much you look forward to seeing her (and dating her) during the summer. Bet you'll get an answer by return mail!

Q. *I am a freshman at a college about one hundred miles from my home town. We have a big dance weekend coming up, and I wrote to invite a girl I used to date. I sent the letter two weeks ago, and still haven't heard from her. The dance is now only three weeks off. How can I tell if she ever got my invitation? And how can I get an answer out of her?*

A. There's a chance, though a small one, that your letter went astray. If you still want the girl to come, drop her another note (this time with your return address clearly written so it will be returned to you if she has moved and left no forwarding address) and reissue the invitation. But give her a deadline to meet. Tell her you need to know by a certain date whether or not she's coming. Give yourself enough leeway to invite someone else if she says "No" or still fails to reply. No answer at all means she couldn't care less (about you or about good manners), so you can tear that page right out of your address book!

Q. *A girl who writes to me at boarding school recently sent a letter with the stamp stuck on upside down. She's never written a single affectionate word to me (we're just good friends), but the guys here tell me she probably meant something by this stamp trick. What do you think?*

A. The upside-down stamp may mean nothing more than that the girl was in a hurry when she mailed the letter. Or she might have resorted to the old, sly subtle way of saying "I love you." Why not wait and see what her next few letters show? If the stamps stay topsy-turvy, you can assume that she didn't just get careless all of a sudden. The gal is trying to tell you something. Are you tuned in?

Q. *I received a typewriter for my birthday, and have found it a wonderful convenience. It's made my homework much easier to do, and I've been getting better grades. I also have stepped up my correspondence, doing all my letter-writing on the typewriter. Now my mother has stepped in and says it's discourteous to type personal letters. I think she's hopelessly old-fashioned.*

A. Your mother isn't hopelessly old-fashioned, just "old school." It used to be considered bad form to type anything other than business letters, and some etiquette purists still insist that bread-and-butter letters and thank-you notes should be penned by hand. But more relaxed rules allow you to answer anything except formal, third-person invitations ("Mr. and Mrs. Jonas Jones request the honor of your presence . . .") by typewriter. The ease and convenience for both sender and receiver far outweigh the slight feeling of impersonality.

Q. *A boy I'm terribly fond of and dated frequently has recently left for the army. We weren't exactly a romance, but we had good times together. He didn't promise to write to me, but he did ask me to drop him a line now and then. I haven't had anything but a post card from him. Would it be all right for me to write to him first?*

A. It's not only all right to drop the fellow a line; it's practically your patriotic duty! For the first few weeks, anyway, he'll be too busy (or exhausted) to scribble more than a line or two. You can keep his spirits up, and his interest in you alive, by writing him once a week, with all the news of home and friends. You're not committing yourself to a lifetime romance, just making sure yours is the first phone number that comes to mind when he gets home on leave.

Q. *I took a girl to a dance when I was home on vacation from school and when I got back to school, I found a letter thanking me for a good time and signed, "Love, Sue." Gee, I'm glad she had fun, but I'm not in the market for any of that love stuff.*

A. Relax! Signing a letter "Love" doesn't mean that the girl thinks you're practically engaged. If she'd closed with "Sincerely," you'd really have something to complain about!

Q. *I'm so embarrassed I could die. The other night I saw my favorite fellow out with another girl. I dashed home and scrawled a furious letter and mailed it without thinking twice. I was hardly back from the corner mail box when he phoned to say he was entertaining his cousin from out* of town and could the two of them drop over. I made some excuse and by now, of course, he's received the letter and will be mad that I didn't trust him. How can I straighten things out?

A. Take to the mail again, apologize for your harsh words and nasty little suspicions. Then hope he'll forgive your jumping to conclusions, which is always a dangerous sport. Next time you're angry and put your thoughts down on paper, be smart enough to wait until the cold light of dawn to reread your message before mailing. If everyone did that, the work of the post office might be cut in half!

Phone Facts

Q. *I'm fifteen and boys are just beginning to call me for dates. But many of the fellows are scared off by my mother's telephone manner. When anyone asks for me, she says, "Who's calling, please?" Sometimes fellows hang up rather than endure the third degree. My mother used to be a secretary before she was married, and I guess she just can't get over the old habits. But it's ruining my date chances.*

A. Explain to your mother that boys in your age group are still shy and unsure of themselves. Ask if she'd just call you to the phone instead of playing social secretary. If she understands that she's frightening off some of your swains, she'll probably change her tactics.

Q. *Do you think it's rude for a girl to say, when a boy phones for a date, "May I let you know tomorrow?" I have to get permission from my mother to accept a date offer (she wants to know where I'm going, with whom and when I'll be home), and when she isn't around to ask, I can't accept. Yet some boys seem to think I'm waiting to see if I get a better offer for the evening.*

A. If a boy thinks he's being brushed off, of course he'll be resentful. You can avoid this by saying, "I'd love to go to the movies (or whatever) but I'll have to check with my mother. Would you call me tomorrow?" This makes it clear that you're not lacking enthusiasm, only parental approval. Since the boy has a set of parents of his own, he'll understand your problem.

Q. *What's a girl supposed to do when a fellow phones and says, "Are you busy Friday night?" without even hinting what plans he has in mind? So many times I've said "Yes" out of pride or because I didn't want to get trapped into something dull. Then I've been sorry later. How can I pry the information out of a prospective date before committing myself?*

A. When a fellow uses the "Are you busy Friday night?" gambit, you may be excused for playing it coy. Say simply, "I'm not sure yet, Jack—why?" Then he'll blurt out his offer and you can make your decision. Don't put your cards on the table until he has his down.

Q. *A boy I date calls me frequently on the telephone and never says who he is. He just assumes that I'll recognize his voice. I don't mean he plays "Guess Who?" games; he simply launches into the conversation, believing I'll know instantly who's calling. This makes me furious. It's as if he's saying, "No other boys ever call you, so of course you know this is me." It seems so conceited of him.*

A. Watch out! Your insecurity is showing. What's wrong with a boy assuming, since he phones you several times a week, that you'll recognize his voice? You wouldn't expect him to reintroduce himself every time you met in the street, and a voice can be as familiar and personal as a face. So climb down off your pedestal (there isn't room for you and the phone up there, anyway) before he feels the chill and stops phoning at all.

Q. *I really need help. I have liked a boy for months. I never dated him but I was so sure I was in love with him that I called him up almost every day for two and a half months. I gave him a false name, but he knew it was really me. Every day I love him more and more, and I know he doesn't like me.*

A. And probably his father doesn't like you, or his mother or the rest of the family who were inconvenienced while you tied up the phone. And who would blame them? You have a typical teen-age crush, except that you're mad about yourself. If you truly like and respect this boy, don't call him again. He has had months to return your calls—if he wanted to.

Q. *The other day I asked a girl for a date for Saturday night and told her I'd phone her Saturday morning to let her know when I'd pick her up. The man I work for weekends sent me on an out-of-town delivery and I didn't get a chance to get to a phone before three o'clock Saturday afternoon. The girl was furious and hung up when she recognized my voice, without even waiting to hear my explanation. Do you think I deserved such rough treatment?*

A. You were guilty of an oversight. The girl gets a black mark for downright rudeness. But she wouldn't have been so upset if she didn't think you were special, so perhaps you'll want to patch things up, even though you got the receiver banged in your ear. Drop her a note, explaining why your call was delayed, and let her take it from there.

Q. *A girl I used to date keeps phoning me all the time and I can't get rid of her. She never rehashes the past or drops any hints that she'd like us to get back together again; she just chats as if she's lonesome. I'd like to brush her off, but nothing seems to work.*

A. You may be polite to listen to the girl's endless phone conversations, but you're not being kind. As long as she believes, because of your patient listening, that she stands a chance of winning you back, she won't leave you alone. Next time she phones (and every time after that), say, "I'm sorry, Jane, but I can't talk to you now." Eventually, she'll get your message, across all those miles of telephone wire.

Q. *The only phone in our apartment is in the living room, so that every conversation has many eager listeners, especially my parents. Whenever by boy friend calls to talk, I don't feel free to exchange mushy small talk. But he gets mad if I don't sign off with "I love you." He just can't seem to understand that I don't like to murmur endearments with three or four people listening. He says my parents know we're going steady and assume we love each other, so I shouldn't be ashamed to say so in front of them.*

A. Let your fellow know, in no uncertain terms, that you consider romance a private affair. If you wanted to shout your devotion from the housetops, you would. But since you prefer to tell only him, then he should love you enough to understand. Just be sure you tell him how you feel about him often enough, when you're alone, to keep his ego at a non-demanding level.

Q. *My name is Tom, and there are six other Tom's in my class. Whenever I phone a girl and say, "This is Tom," she says, "Tom who?" I feel like a goof identifying myself as "Tom Snider"—it seems so formal. And I'd like to think a girl recognizes my voice.*

A. There's nothing for it except to give your full name when you call, until that wonderful day when some special girl recognizes your voice the instant you say "Hello" and gushes, "Tom! I'm so glad you called!" Then you'll know you have it made.

Q. *My girl has a quick temper and hung up on me the other night because I said something that annoyed her. Should I call her back or wait for her to apologize?*

A. Give the girl a chance to simmer down and think second thoughts (including a few about how much she misses you) and let her phone you to apologize. If you phone her as if nothing had happened, she'll never learn that bad temper has its unpleasant results. It's time she learned a lesson, and you can teach it to her!

Q. *The boy I date is a real telephone bug, and phones me every night. It's flattering to have him pay so much attention to me, of course, but I just don't have time to spend half an hour on the phone with him every evening. Besides, I'm beginning to get glares from my parents and older sister, all of whom want to use the phone, too. How can I brush off the boy without hurting his feelings—or his interest in me?*

A. Tell the boy the truth next time he calls. Let him know you enjoy talking to him, but explain that you have to limit your conversation or feel the hot breath of your family down the back of your neck. He'll understand. He's probably getting a few nasty looks around home himself.

Q. *I'm away at school and every now and then I get very lonesome for my girl and want to hear the sound of her voice, so I phone her long distance. Trouble is, she just can't stop talking. She doesn't seem to realize what every word she says is costing me.*

A. Next time you feel the telephone urge, call from a coin telephone. You'll pay for three minutes and when the operator signals that the time is up, you can say quickly, "No more change—by now." Gets you *off* the hook and the receiver back *on.*

Q. *Want the truth? I'm a good-looking fellow and it irritates the girls that I hardly ever date. Whenever there's a hen party, the whole gang calls me up and the gals take turns talking to me. If I make some excuse and hang up, they just ring right back. How do I lick this problem?*

A. Nothing cools the collective ardor of a gaggle of giggling girls faster than a cool maternal voice answering the phone to say, "Charles? No, Charles is out. Who's calling, please?" And to keep your mother an honest woman, go take a walk. It will help clear your head of the sound of female chatter—*and* of the perhaps exaggerated vision you have of yourself as a lady-killer.

Two-Generation Manners

Q. *I work after school and on Saturdays, bagging groceries at the check-out counter of a supermarket. I often see the mothers of girls I've dated when they're shopping in the store. I don't know how to treat them. There just isn't time for small talk.*

A. A big smile and a cheery greeting as you help pack up the vittles is all that's required. Though the mothers might like it if you stopped to chat about their darling daughters, the boss wouldn't. You're supposed to sack groceries; you don't want Boss Man to sack you.

Q. *Whenever I pick up my girl for the evening, her dad starts talking to me about baseball (he knows I'm a big fan) and the conversation drags on so long that my girl gets cross. I don't want to be rude to her father, who seems to be trying hard to put me at ease, but I don't know how to bring the chatter to a close. Any ideas?*

A. When your date comes into the room, stand up. It's the courteous thing to do, and provides a break in the conversation. Once on your feet, you can move toward the door, help the girl with her coat and say good-by to her father, all in one continuing motion.

Q. *Please help me! Both my boy friend and I are in the doghouse. My guy always calls his parents by their first names. He started to address my mother and father the same way and Mom hit the ceiling. When Bob left that night, she told me he should have showed more respect. His mom and dad don't mind; I don't see why mine should object. Mother warned me that if Bob didn't mend his way, I'd have to stop seeing him. Are my parents old-fashioned?*

A. If your beau boy and his parents are on a casual, first-name basis, that's the happy, relaxed arrangement for them. But good manners demand that other adults be addressed more formally. Your parents aren't being old-fashioned in expecting this simple courtesy from your date. Pass the word to Bob; if he doesn't start calling your parents Mr. and Mrs., he's going to have to stop calling you.

Q. *I'm confused about an etiquette rule. When a boy is introduced to the parents of a girl he is dating for the first time, should he shake hands?*

A. Shake hands with her father, but simply acknowledge the introduction to her mother with a polite "How do you do?" And try to say a friendly hello to the assorted small-fry, even if they're climbing up your slacks and clawing at your sport coat. They may answer the phone when you call to leave a message sometime, and you'll want them on your side.

Q. *The boy I go out with has generally good manners, but he never gets up when my parents come into the room when he's there to pick me up for a date. My folks think he's a real hoodlum just because he does this one thing wrong.*

A. Are you sure *you* leap to your feet every time an adult comes into view? A little good example may do the trick. If not, tell Sitting Bull that this small oversight in his etiquette annoys your folks. He's out to please them (or at least to please *you* by getting their approval) and a word to the guys is usually sufficient.

Q. *All the fellows on the basketball team call the coach "Doc." Is this the way to introduce him to my parents?*

A. To you the coach may be Doc or, in private, all sorts of other names. But to your parents, on introduction, he is

"Mr. Jones," with your tone of voice adding a respectful "sir."

Q. *Should a girl remove her glove to shake hands? Sometimes I'm introduced to someone on the street and it's a struggle to get leather gloves off. I'm tired of freezing my fingers just to say "How do you do?"*

A. If you can whip off a glove quickly and gracefully before shaking hands, fine. But don't keep anyone standing and shifting from one foot to another while you peel a hand bare. It's neither insulting nor discourteous to offer a gloved hand promptly.

Q. *When I began to smoke two years ago (at sixteen) my father told me it was good manners to ask, "Mind if I smoke?" before lighting up. I've always done so and always received permission. But when I was visiting a new girl and her family the other night and asked the same old question, her mother said, "I'd rather you didn't." Boy, was I set back on my heels! If I was polite enough to ask, shouldn't she have been polite enough to say O.K.?*

A. The mother may have turned thumbs down on your lighting up because she doesn't like the smell of smoke, because she doesn't believe teens should lay down a smoke screen or because she felt you were setting a bad example for her daughter. Whatever the reason, it's her home and she makes the rules. You asked the question, didn't you? Then you'll have to learn to take "No" for an answer occasionally.

Q. *I know that parents are usually after their teen-aged sons to jack up their manners, but my problem is just the reverse: my folks aren't very polite to my friends. My father almost never rises when my date comes into the room and if I have friends over, my mother barely glances up from her magazine to say "Hello." I'm sure my buddies feel unwelcome in my house, and yet my parents keep urging me to bring friends home. What's the answer?*

A. Maybe you can remind your parents to mind their manners the same way they taught you—by example. If you leap to your feet whenever a female enters the room (yes, even your mother!), your father's courtliness may return. And if you're warm and welcoming to your parents' friends, from your mother's bridge cronies to your father's buddy next door who comes over to play pinochle four nights a week, they may perk up their manners. Give it a try.

Q. *Is it really necessary to ask the female chaperones at a school party to dance? I'm sort of shy and not a very good dancer, and I have a hard enough time asking girls my own age to stumble around the floor with me. When I'm faced with the prospect of dancing with a teacher or the mother of one of my classmates, I really freeze up. But I understand it's the right thing to do.*

A. If you develop two left feet and a bad case of tied tongue when confronted with the chore of dancing with a chaperone, then avoid the situation. Both you and the woman will be too uncomfortable to make the gesture worthwhile. Do be sure, however, at least to greet the chaperone during the evening and say a few pleasant words—about the decorations, the music, the refreshments or how nice it was of her to take the time to oversee the teen fun. She'd probably rather be home watching television or off having a good time with her own age group, so make an effort to let her know she's appreciated.

Q. *I've just entered a new school where the art instructor, a man about fifty-five, is called Mac (his name is McKenzie) by all of his students. He doesn't seem to mind; in fact, I think he welcomes the informality. But I've always been taught to speak very respectfully to teachers (calling them Mr. or sir) and I feel funny using this teacher's nickname. What should I do?*

A. Very often, in an informal course such as art, gym, shop or drama, the teacher has over the years come to be known to students by an affectionate nickname. As long as it's the custom of the school and the instructor seems pleased with the arrangement, go along with the routine. If you started calling your art prof Mr. McKenzie, he'd think you didn't like him!

Q. *In our apartment building, there are many women whom I know by sight as acquaintances of my mother. Sometimes I don't know their names, but I've seen them shopping with my mother or having a cup of coffee in our apartment. I never know how to act when I meet them in the elevator or the lobby of the building. Is a fifteen-year-old guy really supposed to make much conversation with these women? I get the feeling something is expected of me, but I'm not sure what.*

A. Most adults are flattered by *any* conversational attention from teen-agers. Small talk is all that's necessary on these casual encounters and it isn't even essential that you know or call the women by name. "Good morning. It looks as if it's going to be a nice day" or "That's quite a paint job they did in the lobby" or "I hear the management is going to put in self-service elevators next year" will do nicely. Be fast to open doors, step aside to let women in or out of the elevator first, and offer to help with groceries or bundles. The effort will pay off. You'll quickly gain yourself a reputation as "that nice young man on the seventh floor"—and some of those women may turn out to have good-looking, datable daughters just your age!

3 : *The Way You Look*

Face Up!

Q. *I'm sixteen and the only makeup I wear to school is lipstick and a little powder. But I like to wear more makeup on date nights. I haven't had much practice, and no matter how carefully I try to put on my powder base, mascara and eye liner, the effect seems blotched and blurred. Some girls I know wear as much makeup as I do, but it all seems co-ordinated and natural. What am I doing wrong?*

A. You wouldn't expect to learn to paint a beautiful portrait overnight. To do a good job on making up your face, you will need a good deal of practice. Each week your technique will improve and your makeup will be less obvious. The goal is to look your very prettiest and still make people wonder if you're wearing cosmetics at all. Most girls make the mistake of using too much makeup, particularly powder and base. Experiment with thin layers of both, carefully blended, until you're able to apply just enough to cover skin flaws and give your complexion a glow. And use every cosmetic tool available. Invest in a lipstick brush, a good eye liner brush and a small camel hair brush, like a paint-

brush, to flick off excess powder. Practice till you're an expert. And before you go out, check your makeup in a magnifying mirror in a good light. If you can stand the close-up, bright-lights scrutiny, you're ready to face the world.

Q. *I'm dating a very pretty girl, going on seventeen, who doesn't need to wear much makeup to look marvelous. At school she settles for just a little lipstick, but when I take her out to dinner or a dance, she goes all out, including very dramatic eye makeup. My mother has always said that the test of a good cosmetic job is that you can hardly notice it. How can I get my girl to tone down a little, especially the bit with the eyes?*

A. It takes a while for a girl to finish experimenting with new makeup techniques (about fifty years!). All a male can do is flatter her when he likes the way she looks, and be patient and silent when he doesn't. If you criticize your girl, she'll be so defensive she won't bat an eye—*or* remove a single speck of mascara!

Q. *I'm thirteen and very concerned about my looks, like most girls my age. I'm allowed to wear lipstick on state occasions, but I need lots of guidance on how to wear my hair, what clothes are best for me, and so on. Whenever I ask my mother for help, she says, "Handsome is as handsome does" or "I care more about what's inside your head than what's outside it!" The funny thing is that she's pretty and well-groomed herself. I just don't think she's very interested in me.*

A. Maybe you've been "mother's little girl" for so long that she can't take seriously your interest in cosmetics and grooming. Why not save your baby-sitting money and enroll for a good grooming and fashion course at a reputable school (check the Better Business Bureau)? Once your mother realizes you're sufficiently concerned about your appearance to pay out hard-earned cash, perhaps she'll take a greater interest and give you day-to-day tips. Then you'll be ahead two ways.

Q. *I hate girls who primp all the time—and that seems to be all girls. It bothers me to watch a girl put on lipstick or just check her makeup in a compact mirror. Why can't they all pretty-up, and then relax and forget their appearance? I'm sure boys would like it better.*

A. When a girl reaches for her compact, it's to reassure herself that she looks attractive. If you tell her often enough that she's pretty, she won't need to peer into her mirror constantly for confirmation. It's up to you to make her *feel* pretty.

Q. *The other night my boy friend showed up to take me to a dance looking like a hoodlum. He'd forgotten to get a haircut and he really looked raunchy. I told him I wouldn't go with him unless we stopped at a barbershop on the way. He grumbled, but we found a place that stays open late, and he got that haircut. He seemed sulky all evening, and hasn't phoned me since. Was what I did so terrible?*

A. The guy hasn't phoned you since you shepherded him off to the barbershop like a bad little boy. Doesn't that answer your question? And while you're mulling it over, try to figure out why he showed up unshorn in the first place. Have you ever showed up for a date with him with your hair in pincurls under a kerchief, or in unpressed clothes, or with a sloppy makeup job? It's possible that your couldn't-care-less attitude toward appearance rubbed off on him.

Q. *As a special treat for an important party, my mother blew me to a professional hairdo. When it was finished, I looked too fancy and "fixed up" and when I looked in the mirror it didn't seem like me, so, before the party, I stuck my head under the shower and redid my hair on my own. My mother is cross at me for wasting five dollars, plus tip. Should I have gone to the party feeling self-conscious just because the money was spent?*

A. In addition to seeing five dollars going down the shower drain, your mother was probably hurt that her generous gesture didn't come off. If you'd told her on the spot how you felt, you wouldn't have bruised her feelings.

Talk up your gratitude now and your regret that the hairdo didn't work out. She won't stay cross long.

Q. *The girl I'm dating got tired of the way she looked, and last weekend dyed her hair bright red. Frankly, she looks repulsive, and I didn't hesitate to tell her so. Somehow, the hair color doesn't go with her complexion—or with her black eyebrows! She asked me how I liked the dye job and I told her. Now she isn't speaking to me because she says I was unflattering and mean to her. I only told her the truth. Was that so terrible?*

A. Now you know that the truth can hurt, not only the person who hears it but also the person who says it too bluntly. You should have been smart enought to phrase your criticism more kindly. No girl likes to hear that she looks "repulsive," especially if she secretly agrees. Tell her you still like her, even though she has flipped her wig. And then hope she has the good sense to let her natural hair coloring grow back, or at least switches to a less garish tint. No girl should be in a clash by herself!

Q. *I have buck teeth and it spoils my whole appearance. My folks know I'm miserable, but they can't afford the expense of braces. Maybe I'm too proud for my own good, but this is spoiling my whole attitude towart life. Who can smile when he looks like Bugs Bunny?*

A. Check in with a good orthodontist, explain your financial problem and ask if he has any time-payment plan that would allow you to have the dental work done and pay for it out of Saturday job earnings over a period of months. Then find yourself a job and set up the necessary appointments with the dentist. You may have to cut down on date and school and clothes expenditures to meet the bill, but it will be well worth the sacrifice, now and for the rest of your life.

Q. *The boy I date is growing a beard! I simply can't stand to look at him, and think he's doing it only to annoy his parents—and me. I'm afraid to tell him I don't like his chin whiskers, because he's so stubborn that he'd be more eager than ever to raise a bumper crop. I don't know how much longer I can take it.*

A. If your guy has taken to beard-raising as a hobby and you're convinced "he only does it to annoy because he knows it teases," then just ignore his beard—and hope that it will go away! Don't comment on it one way or another unless he asks you directly; then admit, unemotionally, that you don't like his Vandyke. As soon as he realizes that his tickly chin adornment doesn't really bug you, he'll take a good long look at himself in the mirror one morning and presto! a clean-shaven, clean-cut character will emerge again.

Q. *Maybe I'm an old-fashioned guy and am really looking for a girl "just like the girl who married dear old dad." But I'm sick to death of girls with the "morgue" look. All the girls in our school dote on heavy black eye makeup, pale lipstick and black leotards. They come to class looking like fugitives from Charles Addams cartoons.*

A. You can't fight fashion all by yourself. Girls experiment constantly with all sorts of makeup techniques, trying to find the face fashion that suits them best. They're also crowd-followers, and only a very brave and confident girl dares to buck the trend in clothes or cosmetics. But fashion changes.

You'll simply have to be patient until girls decide to look like girls again.

Q. *Please don't laugh at me. I know boys aren't supposed to care too much about how they look, but I'm very concerned about my appearance. My nose is huge, way out of proportion to the rest of my face. I've been begging my parents to let me have plastic surgery, but they won't even discuss it. I'm fourteen and, of course, I can't get an operation without their approval—and their money. How can I convince them I'm serious about this?*

A. Give the rest of your face time to catch up to your nose. The fact is that in adolescence, bodies grow irregularly. Hands and feet are suddenly outsized, noses or ears may look too big for a face. But a schnozz that seems enormous now will probably be just right for your face when you're through growing. Give nature a chance to correct the mistake you think it has made. If, at twenty-one, you still think you need a nose bob, you're on your own.

Q. *I'm sixteen, a football player—and putty in the hands of my girl—up to a point, that is. I have a brownish-blond crewcut and, suddenly, she has taken into her head that she'd like me better really blond and wants me to bleach my hair with peroxide. My parents would be livid, and the guys would never let me hear the end of it. But my girl won't stop nagging me. Do you see any way out?*

A. Tell your girl to get herself a paper doll to call her own, because you're not willing to play the part. You're the man in the twosome. Act like it. Say "No" and mean it—or say "Good-by."

Q. *I'm one of those snaggle-toothed characters who has to wear braces. I'm fifteen, and I have at least another year ahead of the metal contraptions. I didn't mind so much with the kids I've grown up with, but a super new boy has just moved to town and shown an interest in me. He's taken me out twice, and last time asked me if I wasn't having fun, because he'd never seen me smile. I want to skip the whole teeth-straightening project. I'd rather have crooked teeth— and this fellow.*

A. One of the signs of maturity is measuring present inconvenience against future benefits. The new beau boy isn't going to be frightened off by your tooth harness. Best thing to do: grin and wear it!

Q. *I'm a girl of the type known as "black Irish," with a luxuriant head of black hair and more than a sprinkling of same on my upper lip. I hate it. What's the solution?*

A. Bleaching may help, and waxing is a satisfactory, though temporary, answer to your problem. Why not investigate permanent removal with electrolysis? Ask your doctor to recommend the best place to have it done. Sample rates at a good beauty parlor: $7.50 to $10 a half hour. Not a bad way to spend your baby-sitting earnings, since it will improve your appearance and your ego immeasurably.

Q. *I'm fifteen, my mother is thirty-six and very pretty. One reason she looks so attractive is that she wears quite a lot of makeup. But when I try experimenting with eye makeup or tinting my hair, she cracks down. Why should she be so tough on me, when much of her beauty comes out of boxes and bottles?*

A. At thirty-six (which is old, old, old by teen standards!) your mother needs more help from beauty preparations than you do. You agree she is attractive. Why not give her credit for being knowledgeable about makeup and ask her advice on what would be the most flattering—and appropriate—for you? You'll be getting help from an expert with many years of experience before the mirror!

Q. *I'm a boy fifteen, with a big problem I can't face— my face! I have about the worst complexion you've ever seen, and nothing seems to help. My mother said I should get more sleep, watch my diet and drink plenty of water. That didn't help. Neither did special medicated soap, or cold showers, or any of the other home remedies I've tried. Do you have any suggestions? I want to ask girls for dates, but who'd go out with a mess like me?*

A. You wouldn't try to take out your own appendix; why try doctoring a bad skin, which is a medical problem, yourself? Off to the family doctor with you, to get some advice or to be sent to a dermatologist. Great strides have been made in treating acne (there's a lotion containing cortisone, for instance, that has worked wonders with tough cases), and it's foolish to fool around with home cures instead of going to an expert. Once you've started your treatment, don't wait for a complete cure to begin dating. Your self-confidence will increase when you know you've done something constructive about your problem. And girls will be sympathetic about your troubles. You must have noticed that some of them are pretty spotty, too.

Q. *I have an awful problem. I did a terrible thing. I bleached my hair—or, at least, I tried to. My hair is naturally dark brown and I put bleach on it, thinking it would* bring out the highlights. I got impatient when nothing happened and put way too much on. In the morning, my hair was a shocking orange all over. It looked repulsive. My mother says it's all my fault and serves me right for fooling around. I have avoided all my girl friends, but have an important date on Saturday that I can't (and don't want to) break. Please help!

A. Tell your mother you'd rather *dye* than see your guy like this. Then dip into your piggy bank and hie yourself to the town's best hairdresser to have your head repaired. Do something this kooky again and you should have your head *examined!*

Q. *On an impulse last week, I had my hair chopped off very short. I was sick of going to the beach and spending every evening washing the sand out of my hair. I think I look sort of racy and interesting, but my boy friend blew his top when I cropped mine. He says he feels as if he's "going out with the fellows" on date nights. Do you think I should let it grow again to please him? Frankly, I'm delighted with the simple care the new hairdo demands, and most of my friends think it's flattering.*

A. If the future of your romance hangs by a hair—let it grow!

Q. *I have a real problem that I have to face every morning: at sixteen, I need to shave each day and I also have a very bad complexion. Each day my face burns and stings and the eruptions never get a chance to heal. I just don't know how to lick the trouble.*

A. Some adolescent boys with your problem have found that a rotary electric razor, used lightly and kept scrupulously clean, causes less trouble than a blade razor. But you'd be wise to go to a good dermatologist for expert advice on shaving technique and medication. Don't suffer in silence any longer. Tell your troubles to a pro.

Q. *The boy I'm dating has always had brownish blond hair. Lately it seems to me that it's lighter than it used to be and I think he's bleaching it. But whenever I ask him about it, he just blushes and avoids the question. How can I find out the truth?*

A. Why are you so determined to know? Maybe the boy *did* bleach his hair as an experiment or a gag or just because he happened to feel like it. Haven't you ever done anything slightly goofy that you hoped no one would notice or remind you about? Stop nagging and needling; it's time you got out of your fellow's hair, bleached or unbleached.

Q. *I have a sweet tooth, plus a bad complexion and a dumpy figure. I know one trouble can lead to others, but I just can't get the money together to see a doctor. My mother says she'll pay half the bill if I can manage to scrape together enough cash to pay the other half. What can I do? I feel like such a mess—and desperate.*

A. Try a two-month home cure. Put every dime and quarter you want to spend on goodies for that sweet tooth right into a piggy bank. No soft drinks today, no candy bar after lunch tomorrow, no fudge sundae after the movies with the girls next Saturday night. Don't expect miracles, but by the time that piggy bank is filled, you probably won't *need* the doctor.

Q. *I never feel really "dressed" without lipstick, and if I don't wear it, my lips feel dry and uncomfortable. My girl*

friends tease me about wearing it, even at a pajama party
or at summer camp. They say I'm boy-crazy, even when
there are no boys around.

A. When you look pretty, you feel better. So go right
ahead and wear lipstick, even to bed if you feel like it. Just
close your ears to the needling of your friends. Lipstick
wouldn't go well with their green eyes, anyway!

Q. *It seems to me that my skin breaks out more frequently*
when I'm under pressure or am upset. If I have a big test
coming up or a boy asks me to a special dance and I get all
excited, my face begins to act up. My mother says I'm just
imagining this.

A. Part of adolescent skin troubles are due to physio-
logical changes, part to faulty diet and health habits and,
most experts agree, part to emotional upsets. If you're excited or worried, your skin is likely to show it. What can
you do about it? Relax as much as possible. Try to roll with
the punch and realize that this is a part of growing up.
Once you've checked your diet, your cleanliness routine and
your sleep habits, and used whatever medication and cover-
up lotion your doctor recommends, think about your complexion as little as possible. It's one of those problems which,
if you ignore it and hope it goes away, often does, simply
because you've stopped stewing.

It Figures

Q. *I wish you could help me. My family and my doctor*
have tried, but, so far, no luck. I'm overweight by about
twenty pounds, and I know it. Underneath the layers of fat I
have a pretty enough face, and a potentially good figure.
But I'm just too heavy to be attractive to boys. Whenever

*the other girls have dates, I get very lonesome and blue,
and then I eat to get over feeling sorry for myself. Its' really
a vicious circle, and I can't break it.*

A. At least you recognize your compulsive eating pattern,
and that's the first step toward correcting it. Get a carefully
worked out diet from your doctor and promise yourself
you'll stick to it for a week. It's not so hard to strengthen
your will power for short stretches at a time. Whenever
you're feeling sorry for yourself and head for the refrigerator, stop dead in your tracks and determinedly do
something else to cheer up: tune in a good TV show, go off
to a movie (closing your eyes as you pass the popcorn
machine!), check through your closets and bureau drawers
for clothes that need mending, settle down with a mystery
story that engrosses you completely. When your will power
needs bolstering, nibble on a carrot stick or have a no-
calorie soft drink while you remind yourself of the advan-
tages of being thinner—the facts that you'll look better in
clothes, be more attractive to boys, feel more energetic.
Once you've managed to get through one week, the next
week will be easier, and, eventually, you'll be able to break
the fat-because-you're-unhappy, unhappy-because-you're-fat
cycle.

Q. *I'm a sixteen-year-old guy, built like a telephone pole.
I've been invited to a swimming party by a girl I like a lot.
I haven't accepted yet, because I can't stand the idea of
being seen (especially by her) in bathing trunks. Everyone
will laugh at my knobby knees and skinny chest. I'd die
rather than face that.*

A. The girl never suspected there was a Mr. America
lurking under the sports shirts and slacks—nor does she care
much, or she wouldn't have invited you to the party. Many

teen-age boys are built along bean pole lines, but they don't hide until they fill out their muscles. Go to the party, enjoy yourself and, incidentally, take a silent poll on how many other guys there have similar problems. If it will make you feel better, buy a terry cloth pullover to wear pool-side. A few more swimming parties will do you good. There's no exercise better for building up those chest muscles!

Q. *I'm a fifteen-year-old girl and haven't yet begun to develop a figure. I asked my doctor about my problem, and he just says that I'm a "late bloomer" and not to worry. But he doesn't have to face the giggles and teases from the other girls about my boyish figure. My mother is reluctant to give me permission to wear padded bras. What do you think?*

A. You can bolster your ego, and your figure, by giving nature a nudge. Teen-age lingerie departments stock brassieres that are discreetly padded. Show these to your mother. I'm sure she will agree that, as long as you stay away from the synthetic Jayne Mansfield models, these are a wise investment for a self-conscious teen more worried than the State Department about "underdeveloped areas." A little head start is better than agonizing over "too little, too late" in the figure department.

Q. *Our school has been concentrating heavily on a physical fitness program. At least one gym period a week is devoted to calisthenics and tumbling, and now the gym teacher has announced we're going to have a demonstration of what we've learned for parents. I could just die. I'm fifteen pounds overweight, look like a sack in my gym suit and just can't face appearing in public, although I'm good at all the exercises, considering my size. I've asked to be excused, but the coach says "No dice." How can I ever face people?*

A. If you're really dissatisfied with your appearance, facing this audience shouldn't be more shattering an experience than facing your mirror each morning. Maybe the embarrassment will be just the extra push you need to get a diet from your doctor and stick to it. Combine this with the exercise, and it should be possible for you to pare that poundage in just three months. Wouldn't you really like to try?

Q. *I'm a boy seventeen, good enough looking, I guess, but with very spindly legs. I've always been self-conscious about my lack of muscles and never wear shorts when I'm out with girls unless I absolutely have to. The girl I'm now dating is a tennis whiz and knows I'm on the tennis team at my school, so she's begging me to play with her. But I don't want her to see me in shorts.*

A. If she's such a tennis whiz, she knows enough to keep her eyes on the ball. And that doesn't leave her free to give your legs a second look. So play ball!

Q. *I've met a wonderful guy who doesn't seem to mind that I'm about twenty pounds overweight. He says he likes my personality and that, even though I'd be more attractive if I slimmed down, he likes me well enough just the way I am. Now he's urging me to go to the beach with him, and I haven't gone for the last two summers because I'm too ashamed of my weight. What do you suggest?*

A. Invest some of your baby-sitting savings in the most flattering bathing suit you can buy, as well as a short beach coat. Certainly don't turn down fun offers from a boy who likes you for no other reason than because you're worried about your appearance. Having him see you in a bathing suit may embarrass you into going on a serious diet. By the end of the summer, you could turn into quite a dish—if you stay away from the fattening dishes that got you into trouble in the first place.

Q. *I've exercised, dieted and done everything I can think of to solve my problem, but I still have large, unshapely legs. The rest of my figure is excellent, but it all seems wasted because my legs are so unattractive. Obviously, I can't change them. How can I camouflage them?*

A. If you have any shorts, slacks or tight skirts in your wardrobe, give them away, quickly! Full or eased skirts will be more becoming to you. Buy slightly darker shades of stockings to make your calves look slimmer, but avoid dark gray, blue or black, which will only call attention to your legs. Spike heels are not for you, either, since the needle-type heels provide too sharp a contrast to heavy legs. Medium heels, stacked, are best for girls with your problem. Continued exercise to slim those limbs is essential. Once you've done everything possible to minimize your difficulty, ignore it. If the rest of your figure is excellent, who's really going to look at your legs?

Tip-to-Toe Attractiveness

Q. *Everyone talks about how important it is to be neat and well-groomed to be at your most attractive. But I'd like to know how a girl can achieve a bandbox appearance when there's only one bathroom in an apartment—and six people to share it! I'm lucky if I manage to get my teeth brushed in the morning, to say nothing of getting all glamoured up.*

A. Agreed, good grooming isn't as simple with a six people—one bathroom ratio as it would be if you had your own pink marble tub with gold faucets. But with planning, it *is* possible. Get your bath or shower before bedtime, or get up fifteen minutes before the rest of the family to bathe. After tooth-brushing and wake-up face washing, the rest of your grooming can be done in your bedroom. A fluffy-skirted dressing table would be nice, but a small shelf holding grooming aids and a decent-sized mirror on the wall will do just as well. So stop making excuses—and start making progress in your grooming program.

Q. *Boy, am I bewildered! I've just become seriously interested in my appearance (for the usual reasons—I have a special boy friend). I have no confidence in my ability to choose my own clothes or judge my own makeup and hair style. When I ask my girl friends for their opinions, I get conflicting advice. I'm so mixed up now I don't know what to wear or even how I want to look.*

A. Your gal pals are often the last persons on earth to consult on your appearance. Either they like you so well they'll say you look marvelous, just because they don't want to criticize and hurt your feelings, or they dislike you just enough to resent the competition when you look well and steer you wrong. In any case, it's difficult for someone you know to be objective. Invest some of your baby-sitting money in a course on grooming and hair styling. Let the instructor take a hard, cold look and give you professional advice. Read fashion magazines for your age group, both to find out what's currently fashionable and to discover what's best for your type of face and figure. And study yourself mercilessly in a full-length mirror. In the long run, only you can decide how you want to look. It's a lifetime job; better begin now.

Q. *I'm a boy, seventeen, a good student and a star athlete. Also, I'm considered good-looking and popular. I mention all this to let you know I'm no square. But have I got a complaint about girls! Why do girls spend so much time and effort choosing the right clothes and hair style, grooming themselves perfectly, and then spoil the whole effect by chewing gum like Eskimos softening sealskin for boots? I saw three girls on the street today who looked like real dishes, but I lost interest in them when I saw their jaws working like pistons. Won't someone please set females straight on the advantage of being feminine?*

A. There you are, gals. A word from the guys should be sufficient!

Q. *My girl friend is blind as a bat without her glasses, yet she won't wear them on dates. I've seen her in them every day since we were both freshmen in high school (we're now seniors) and I think she looks pretty in them, but she's too vain to wear them when I take her out at night. So she stumbles into things, doesn't recognize friends who say hello, and squints across the table at me so she doesn't look nearly as pretty as when wearing her specs. I'm sort of tired of being her Seeing Eye boy. How can I make her realize she's being foolish?*

A. If she won't wear her glasses, it's because she doesn't really believe she looks attractive in them. It's up to you to convince her, through a concentrated campaign of flattery,

that she's actually prettier in her blinders than without them.
Here's a chance to test your powers of persuasion.

Q. *Boys are always complaining about girls who put on
lipstick in public. But how about boys who are constantly
combing their hair? I date one boy who pulls the comb out
of his back pocket about every ten minutes. This drives me
wild. I wish he'd get a crewcut.*

A. Tell him his public grooming irritates you and ask him,
politely, to stop. He'll either stop combing his hair—or stop
dating you.

Q. *Many of us guys are disgusted by the day-to-day ap-
pearence of most girls. For dates or dances, they get all
dressed up and made up like Hollywood starlets. But they
come to school looking like frumps, with wrinkled clothes,
sloppy makeup, stringy hair. Sometimes it's almost impossible to recognize the girl you were out with the night
before. Don't they have any pride?*

A. Girls have pride, all right, but sometimes it needs a
little prodding from fellows like you. Smart girls will put up
their hair before falling into bed and get up fifteen minutes
earlier in the morning to do a decent, all-day makeup job.
It may require special effort to look marvelous for an 8:45
class—but that's where the boys are!

Q. *When I'm nervous, the palms of my hands get all hot
and perspire-y. This is especially bad when I dance with a
girl. Isn't there anything I can do about it?*

A. Try rubbing your hands with a light men's cologne
before leaving on a date, or dusting with an anti-perspirant

powder. Either of these devices will help. Best solution of all is further date experience and increased self-confidence. Once your nervousness disappears, so will the symptoms.

Q. *Maybe you'll think I'm a fuddy-duddy, but I don't like my girl to ask me to rub her with sun lotion when we're on the beach. It seems to me very intimate and it embarrasses me. But how can I say "No" to her when I know she gets beet-red if she doesn't use some sort of sun-screening cream or lotion?*

A. Invest in sun lotion in an aerosol can. You can spray her back without the whole routine seeming so *intime,* and for the rest—she can be a do-it-herself type.

Q. *I'm a flaming redhead, and freckle madly and burn to a crisp when I'm out in the sun. I also like to swim and love lolling around the beach with my pals. But since I look like a speckled lobster after one afternoon, boys never give me a second look. Any suggestions, other than huddling under a beach towel all day?*

A. How come you haven't yet discovered the marvelous sun creams, which screen out *all* the rays of the sun, and make beach life safe and fun for sun-haters? Check with your drugstore or department store for one of the several brands. You may also choose to wear a beach hat (there are so many wild and wonderful ones that you can turn your need into an asset) and cover-up skirt when you're not swimming, so you don't have to spend half the day smearing yourself with protective cream. Hustle off to the drugstore; only a zombie would hide from June to September, when there's all that fun to be had.

Q. *A girl I date is a bug about her fingernails. You'd think she was raising prize orchids the way she concentrates on growing nails long as talons. She won't go bowling or play tennis in case she breaks one of her precious nails. The night she snagged one on my sweater when we were dancing, I thought the roof would fall in. I don't know what to make of her.*

A. Try making her an ex-date. If she's so enamored of her nails that she limits her date fun, strike her off your list. You have ten rivals, and that's too much to cope with.

Q. *The girl I date has one terrible habit that irritates me and embarrasses me, but I don't know what to do about it without making her angry or hurting her feelings. If we go out to eat, when we finish she redoes her whole makeup at the table: powder, lipstick, hairdo, the whole bit. I sit and fidget and look the other way and try to pretend I'm not with her, but I'm seething inside.*

A. A discreet application of lipstick at the table is permissible, but any grooming repairs beyond that belong in the privacy of the ladies' room. Next time your girl begins a facial retread, try saying lightly, "I thought you just *happened* to be pretty—you're ruining all my illusions." If she doesn't scurry for cover, she needs a new set of sensibilities, or you need a new girl!

Q. *A boy I date is a hot rod fiend, and though he's well-groomed in every other way, his hands always look terrible because grease is ground into the creases of his skin and his nails are never really clean. I suppose this is a small complaint, but I've always admired nice hands on men, and it's disappointing to find this flaw in a boy I like so much.*

A. A handsome case of manicure implements for his birthday or graduation might be just the hint to turn the trick. But don't press your luck. If you ask the boy to choose between his greasy car and you—the car is likely to win!

Q. *Could you suggest a good, simple grooming routine for a teen-aged girl who wants to look her best?*

A. Schedule a bath or shower every day, and wash your face as soon as you get up in the morning and before you go to bed at night. A noon-time fresh-up at school, using a lotion-moistened paper towel which comes in a foil packet, improves your appearance and refreshes you for the afternoon ahead. Teeth-brushing morning and night; also at noon if you get home for lunch. Shampoo weekly, more often if needed. Hair-setting as frequently as your coiffure requires. Manicure once a week, touch up polish between times when needed. Shave your legs and underarms the instant they need it. And at least once a week, spend a pampering hour putting yourself in shape for the days ahead. Pluck your eyebrows if necessary. Rub your face with cream or lotion and soak for half an hour in a sudsy tub, redolent with bath oil. Use pumice stone on your elbows and heels and any other rough spots. Finish off with a splash of cold water and a brisk toweling, and you'll emerge looking better and feeling relaxed and marvelous. With your grooming on a regular schedule, ten minutes should be enough to get you ready for the day with a light base, powder and lipstick. And pretty as you are with day-to-day basic care, fifteen minutes should be all you need to get glamoured up for the evening, mascara and all!

Q. *A girl in our crowd is very attractive and well-groomed and is quite hip, except for one thing—she doesn't seem to have heard about deodorants. She's a swell girl, but, frankly, it's not very pleasant to be near her. How can one of us clue her in without offending her?*

A. The girl may be miffed for a moment if one of you simply speaks up, privately and pulling no punches, but eventually she'll be grateful. Make this a case where her best friend *will* tell her.

Q. *I'm supposed to buy my own cosmetics from my allowance, and I have quite a lot invested in medicated soaps, toothpaste, creams, mascara, eye liner, etc. But I can't make my family keep their hands off my things. My parents use my toothpaste, my sister leaves my soap in a sticky puddle in the wash basin, and the crowning blow came when my bratty little brother used my eye liner brush to paint his model airplanes. They just don't respect private property.*

A. Peering through soapy eyes, your family isn't always going to reach for the right toiletries in a cluttered medicine cabinet. You could, of course, set aside one shelf in the cabinet for your things and announce a hands-off-or-else policy. But you're still likely to get poachers, especially among the small-fry who aren't as aware of the restrictions on private property as they might be. So, to put an end to the fuss, why not keep all your beauty aids in a cosmetic kit, hatbox or even a large plastic bag (the kind your mother uses to store leftovers in the refrigerator) in your bedroom, toting it to the bath at grooming time? Everything will be in one place—and it's all yours!

Q. *Maybe you'll think I'm a boob for asking a question like this, but I'm a boy who just doesn't seem to know what to do with his hands. I'm tall and gangly anyway, and it*

always seems to me that my hands are just hanging *there.*
So I fidget and pluck at my tie or brush my hair back or
squirm. I'm sure I make everybody nervous just to look at
me.

A. A really poised man can stand with his hands hanging
along the seams of his trousers and look perfectly at ease.
But until you feel more sure of yourself (participation in
athletics will help you to feel more "comfortable" with
your body; time will help even more), try clasping your
hands behind your back or putting them in your jacket
pockets.

4 : *The Way You Dress*

Wardrobe Planning

Q. *I'm a teen-ager, not quite seventeen, and though I keep a sense of humor about my appearance, I know I'm quite pretty. (My mirror tells me I am, and so do my friends.) My main trouble is my clothing. I shop and shop and then get so disgusted with myself and my taste that I end up buying just anything. As a result, most of my wardrobe is a mess. How can I develop some taste and clothes sense?*

A. Taste takes time—and effort—to acquire. Before you buy another thing, read the fashion pages of your newspaper, pick out clothes and models you admire in magazines and ads, set aside a Saturday afternoon or two for viewing fashion shows at department stores. Decide what you like and what would probably be right for you. Check your opinion with a good friend whose style sense you admire.

Then go over your current wardrobe. Keep the things that fit in with your new picture of yourself, give the others away. It's no economy to wear unbecoming clothes just "because they're there." Better to wear just two or three outfits which flatter you during a week than to dress differently, but unattractively, every day.

Also, change your shopping habits. Have a fairly firm idea of what you want before you head for the stores, so you won't be muddled into buying an unnecessary date dress or an expensive accessory that doesn't fit into your wardrobe. Plan for a shopping trip as carefully as you would for an important date. Too many teen-agers shop when they are tired, badly groomed, loaded down with schoolbooks—and then wonder why the mirror doesn't reflect a glamourous image. Do your shopping when you're fresh-faced, girdled, high-heeled and looking your best. Then you won't be so likely to be "discouraged" into making bad choices. When you've tried an outfit on in front of a three-way mirror and are quite sure you like it, ask the salesgirl to put it aside for half an hour. If the purchase still seems like a good idea after you've mulled it over and checked it out against your current wardrobe needs and your image of yourself, it probably is.

Q. *How much attention do you think a girl should pay to her fellow's taste in clothes—girls' clothes, that is? I've always liked fashion and spent a lot of time and care on my wardrobe, which I think is just right for me. And I have the reputation of being well dressed. But the boy I go with is forever pointing out dresses in store windows that he thinks he'd like on me. I know they'd be wrong for me, but I wonder if I should buy one or two of them to please him.*

A. You won't be happy or comfortable in clothes that you don't think are right for you, no matter how much flattery they draw from your fellow friend. So stick to your own taste, in spite of what your beau boy says, without rejecting his judgment too obviously. ("It *is* a pretty dress—maybe I'll get one like it when I've saved enough.") You can't change wardrobes every time you change beaus—your budget would never stand the strain.

Q. *I'm a girl, fifteen, who has just realized the dream of a lifetime—and it doesn't seem worth the effort. After three months of careful dieting under the eye of my doctor, I've finally lost the extra fifteen pounds I've been carrying around with me ever since I was eleven. But now my clothes are all so big for me that I look as awful as ever—and I can't afford a whole new wardrobe. I'm so discouraged I could cry. Losing the weight took so much effort and energy that I just didn't plan ahead to what I'd wear.*

A. Many of your clothes can be tailored satisfactorily to fit your new figure. Skirts can be taken in, blouses can be tapered from armpit down to look trimmer—and sweaters can be a little baggy without looking terrible. If your mother isn't handy with a needle, perhaps you can trade services with a neighbor. Offer to baby-sit or do household chores in exchange for some friendly tailoring. But you need some new clothes in addition to your altered things. Ask for an advance on your allowance or step up your baby-sitting activities to finance the purchase of two or three outfits that really fit and flatter. You deserve to reward yourself for all the effort of the past three months. It's important not to stall on revamping your wardrobe. If you continue to look baggy and unkempt, you could become so discouraged that you'd allow yourself to get pudgy all over again.

Q. *The girl I go with is very critical of my appearance and I'm getting tired of being told that I ought to get a haircut or that my tie isn't tied right or that my sweater doesn't go with my slacks. She's a swell girl, neat as a pin herself, but I never wanted to be a fashion plate, and I don't intend to start now. How can I let her know that her harping is getting on my nerves?*

A. Whipping beau boys into shape is a favorite hobby of girls. And maybe there's something to what your severest critic says. You say she's always well turned out, so she's probably more of an expert on personal appearance than you are. Instead of taking offense, why not take her hints and get into the habit of good grooming and careful clothes choice? You'll undoubtedly look better. And isn't it easier to get the friendly word from her than from a hoped-for boss later on, who says you just don't *look* right for the job?

Q. Our family doesn't have much money and I'm worried about my clothes when I go into senior high school next month. What is the absolute minimum a girl can get by with?

A. Whether the cash comes out of the family budget or your earnings from a part-time job, you'll need certain basic essentials. Starting from the skin out, you'll have to have three changes of underthings, a lightweight panty girdle (with removable garters), two skirts (one solid color, one patterned), three blouses (two tailored, one slightly more dressy for Sundays or movie evenings), two sweaters (one cardigan, one pullover), five pairs of socks, loafers or other simple flat shoes, a pair of medium-heeled dress shoes, two pairs of hose, one simple party dress that can be changed by varied accessories (jewelry, scarves, etc.), a pair of short white gloves, one all-purpose coat, a handbag, a string of pearls and a pair of blue jeans or slacks for knockabout home wear, to save your school clothes. Buy your basic wardrobe in the same color spectrum, so that everything can be switched around, mixed and matched, to get the maximum wear from each. As soon as you can scrape up the cash, add a simple, well-tailored suit and one pair each of slacks and shorts (if your figure rates them). Hats aren't necessary when the budget is tight; a snug little tie-on veil will take you to church or wherever else hats are usually required. Each time you add something extra to your wardrobe, think carefully how it will fit in with the clothes you already own. If it doesn't mesh smoothly or if the purchase means buying a whole new set of accessories to make it look right, then pass it up, no matter how tempting. Fashion on a budget requires planning, careful shopping and great self-discipline.

Q. *I like to wear very bright-colored sport shirts for school. But my girl says I look too jazzy. Most men have to wear such conservative clothes once they go into business that I figure I might as well have my fun while I can. Who's right?*

A. Bright colors in sport shirts are fine; bizarre colors, no! A snappy plaid, good-looking stripes or an all-over pattern can be great, as long as the color combination doesn't knock your eye out. If a shirt shouts, "Hey, look!" then put it right back on the counter and buy something less flamboyant. Watch out for wild color combinations. A pale blue shirt is fine; a blue striped with lavender and lime is murder. Patterns which are too busy and colors which are too garish are a mistake, especially for teen-aged boys with skin problems. A combination of too many colors or too cluttered a pattern only seems to emphasize spotty skin, adding up to too much for the eye to absorb. A few additional hints: always wear shirttails tucked in unless they're straight-bottomed shirts, designed for in-or-out wear, and even then, you'll look better with them tucked in. Unless you're wearing a tie, leave the top button of any shirt unbuttoned. Finally, if you're wearing a tie, *wear one*, not a skinny little string substitute, with a sliding clasp, like something out of a second-rate Western. Try to learn the difference between "sharp" and "smart." It'll take a while; let your girl help you learn.

Q. *At sixteen, I'm finally allowed to shop for my own suits and sport coats. Before now, my dad has always gone with me, and he's made sure the alterations were correct. I'm pretty sure of my taste in colors and fabrics, but I freeze up when the guy with the chalk starts fooling around with the length of the sleeves and trousers. When he says, "Is that the way you want it, sir?" I just want to get out of there fast, before he gets wise to how stupid I am.*

A. If you're shopping in a good store with a fine reputation for men's fashions, you can leave the decision up to the tailor—he knows what's right. Here's a good rule of thumb, however: a jacket sleeve should be just long enough to allow about half an inch of shirt cuff to show when your arms are hanging at your side, and trouser cuffs should just brush the top of the shoe in front, making a slight "break" in the crease, so the trousers don't hang board-stiff.

Q. *I never know how long to make my skirts. Every time fashion changes, I go into a swivet, worrying about how the new length of dresses will look on me. I don't have good legs, and when I wear skirts as short as is sometimes fashionable, I look cut off and stumpy.*

A. Good taste is what looks right for you, so don't let your spirits go up and down with the hemlines. If you have a leg problem, your skirts should always cover your knee-cap, no matter where the current fashions hit the perfectly proportioned legs of models. Settle on the length that looks best on you, judging yourself in front of a full-length three-way mirror. When you feel that you look right, you can be pretty sure that you do.

Q. *Even though I'm a fifteen-year-old fellow, my mother picks out all my clothes for me, from undershirts to sport coats. I guess I should be grateful that she also picks up the tab (some of my friends have to earn their clothes money), but she and I have entirely different taste. Most of the fellows in my class wear sport shirts and chinos to school; I look like a banker in my button-down shirts and gray flannel slacks. Whenever I mention to my mom that I'd like to pick out my own clothes or at least go along and have some say in the decision, she says I can choose them when I can afford to buy them. What's a way out?*

A. A fifteen-year-old boy can't be well-dressed when he's wearing apron strings. Maybe you can work out a compromise: your mother still picks out your clothes but you have veto power. If not, do as she suggests. Get a Saturday job which will finance your own clothes purchases. You're bound to make mistakes as you build your own wardrobe, and sometimes you'll make purchases that will turn your mother's hair a brighter shade of gray. But you'll be learning —about men's fashions and the financial facts of life. And your mother will be learning that a fifteen-year-old is striving for and needs more and more independence.

Q. *I'm a sixteen-year-old girl, five feet four inches tall and weigh 112 pounds. I don't seem overweight, but I do have a tummy problem. No matter how hard I try to keep my posture good, my stomach sticks out. Do you think I should wear a girdle every day? It seems like a lot of trouble.*

A. Even if weight isn't a problem, a girdle is often necessary to give your figure a disciplined, "organized" look. Invest in two or three lightweight panty girdles for school wear. You'll feel better put together, and have a lovelier profile all the way down.

Q. *What basic wardrobe do I need for my sophomore year in a boys' high school? I've outgrown all last year's clothes and we can't afford to spend much because dad has been laid off work for a while.*

A. You'll need five changes of underwear, two pairs of chinos (preferably three), a pair of dark flannel slacks, five sport shirts, one white dress shirt and a conservatively patterned tie, a sweater, five pairs of athletic socks, one pair of dark socks for dress-up, loafers, a sport coat and a coat which will double for school and dress wear (a finger-tip suburban in plain fabric or muted pattern, or a blue or loden duffle coat is a good choice). As soon as possible, add a dark gray flannel suit for big dates and church; the pants can double as extra slacks with your sport coat. With these items in your closet, kept clean and well-pressed, you can be well-dressed on a budget.

Clothes Horse Sense

Q. *I've got plenty of clothes, maybe too many. My problem is not fashion, but organization. Everything's all jumbled together in my closet and bureaus, and even if the outfit I put on goes together, it usually looks rumpled and mussed.*

I spend a lot on cleaning and pressing, but it's a waste of time with the small closet tacked to my bedroom. What'll I do? We can't move to a bigger place.

A. You have put your own finger on it—you lack organization. And only you can bring order out of your closet chaos. Decide to do it this weekend. Turn down a Friday night date offer, just to put the pressure on yourself to get the job done. First, give away any clothes you haven't worn in a year. If they didn't fit into your life in the last twelve months, it's unlikely you'll develop a sudden new passion for them. Dip into your savings for closet accessories; you'll save the price in pressing bills within the month. Buy hangers with clips for skirts and clamp wooden hangers for slacks and shorts. You'll need a shoe rack for the floor of the closet or a shoe bag to hang inside the door. If you have an assortment of handbags, a purse caddy, which hangs from the closet pole and cradles each purse in its own fabric compartment, keeps your bags free from dust and scuffing, and close at hand. Hang each type of clothing together. Fragile or little-worn clothes go into zippered garment bags, or get shrouded with an old shirt of your father's. To make extra room, hang an additional pole just far enough above the existing rack to accommodate blouses and jackets. You can also get a light metal rack for hangers that extends out from the inside of a closet door. It will hold up to a dozen dresses! And at least once a week, go through your closet to neaten things, make sure clothes are hung carefully on hangers, and sort out what needs cleaning or washing or mending.

The same ruthless organization applies to your bureau, too. First sort out and discard. Then make drawer dividers out of lengths of cardboard covered with decorative self-adhesive plastic. Tape them upright to the inside front and back of the drawers, to keep gloves from sliding into handkerchiefs, to separate petticoats from half slips. If your bureau drawers are so deep that you must rumple through several layers of clothes to get at what you want, cut cardboard sheets slightly smaller than drawer size and use them, tray fashion, between layers of different types of clothes, so you can lift out an entire "tray" of lingerie, for instance, to get at sweaters. Your jewelry goes into a series of small boxes, into a compartmented silverware tray from the dime store or in one of the many-drawered plastic chests sold at hardware store or notion counters.

If you're still short of storage space, think about zippered plastic storage boxes, made like suitcases, which slip under your bed; ideal for storing out-of-season or little-used clothing. They are around four dollars at department stores. Also available are black steel racks which hold brightly painted fiberboard boxes that are ideal containers for all sorts of clothes and oddments. A rack and nine boxes, each 10" by 11" by 11", stacked three high and three across, comes to less than eleven dollars—and worth every penny.

Q. *I'm going to our senior prom next month and the boys are all expected to wear white dinner jackets. I don't own one and don't know where to borrow one to fit me. I've been told you can rent these outfits for the evening, but I don't know where. And I certainly can't afford to blow dough on buying something so expensive that I'll wear one night— and probably outgrow before I ever get a chance to wear it again.*

A. Check the classified telephone directory under "Dress Suit Rental" for the shop in your town that will turn you

into an instant fashion plate. But remember that there'll be a big rush on formal attire during the prom season, so do go in now. Try on white dinner jackets and reserve one for the big night without further delay.

Q. *I'm fifteen and my mother says it's time a girl my age started to be responsible for taking care of her own clothes. Up till now, everything's always been clean and ironed and waiting for me in my bureau or closet. I don't know where to begin.*

A. Sounds as if your mother is trying to teach you to swim by throwing you off the dock. Before you take over your clothes care, ask your mother for a short, intensive course in laundering and ironing. Most of your clothes can probably still be tossed in with the family wash, though you should be responsible for squeezing out your hosiery and under-things and anything else that requires special hand care. Have your mother outline to you what things in your ward-robe require sprinkling before ironing, and which fabrics can best be touched up with a steam iron. Have her teach you the most efficient and speedy way to iron each type of garment, which fabrics among those you plan to wash can be bleached, etc. Make a mental note or, better still, type up a chart to hang near the washing machine or clothes hamper, and fill in new information as new items are added to your wardrobe. Once you've absorbed the how-to info, stop grumbling and grousing and get to work. You're a big girl now. You've been lucky to escape laundry chores for as long as you have.

Q. *I've always admired a certain bunch of guys at our school. They're popular and run things and are always sharp dressers. A few weeks ago the whole crowd began wearing gray slacks, blue blazers, white shirts and black knit ties. I thought they looked pretty snappy and bought the same sort of outfit for myself. But yesterday three of them took me aside and told me it was the uniform of their club and I should butt out. Don't I have the right to wear whatever clothes I want to?*

A. You can, of course, wear whatever clothes you choose. But since you admire these fellows and hope to have them as friends (or at least not as enemies), better not try to muscle your way into their charmed circle. To be a member of the crowd, you'd have to do a lot more than ape their attire. Better save that blue blazer for date nights, buy yourself a different kind of tie and settle down with your own circle of friends. Although to you imitation may seem the sincerest form of flattery, these fellows aren't flattered—only irritated.

Q. *My girl thinks she's some sort of sexpot. All her clothes are tight-fitting and slinky and low-cut. I can't figure this out, because she's actually rather shy and retiring. She blushes if anyone tells an off-color joke, and I went with her for six months before she'd let me kiss her good night. In fact, she's so shy that I can't even bring up the subject of her come-hither clothes. I'm baffled.*

A. Most girls go through a period of experimentation with clothes, trying to find what's right for their personality and figure. Some girls choose clothes that reflect themselves as they *are*, some as they'd *like* to be. Perhaps your girl selects sexy, look-at-me clothes because she is shy and would rather be a *femme fatale*. Help her by admiring her when she looks as you like her to look, commenting casually on clothes you like—on other girls, in store windows, in magazines and newspapers. Then just go on hoping that eventually she'll recognize her true type—and dress to fit it.

Q. *I go out with a girl who is a lot shorter than I am, and whenever we dance close, I get lipstick on the lapel of my jacket. I'm tired of having to pay the cleaning bills out of my small allowance, and yet I don't like to complain to the girl. Do you have any good ideas?*

A. Instead of having your whole jacket cleaned, do a spot job on the lipstick stains with a do-it-yourself cleaner just before you leave for your date. A good solid whiff of cleaning fluid will make your girl turn her head aside when you dance together—and maybe even jog her memory about where you got the spot in the first place. She doesn't have to put her brand on you just because you're her best dance partner.

Who Wears What Where

Q. *What do you think of jeans for boys for school? We're allowed to wear whatever clothes we want for classes, and jeans are a nice, cheap way for a fellow to dress.*

A. If many other fellows wear jeans to school, you can probably get away with them, as long as they're not low-slung and hip-hugging. But chinos or khakis are about on a par in price with jeans, and they are much trimmer and dressy-looking. They can take you anywhere—from classes, to the after-school hangout, to shopping trips downtown, to casual dates. So you would probably end up saving money in the long run.

Q. *I've been invited to two different Christmas formals by two different boys, though the crowd will be about the same at both dances. I have only one winter formal dress and my mother says the budget won't stretch to buy me another. I hate to show up wearing the same dress at both parties. Do you think this is silly of me?*

A. Yes! You'll be wearing different accessories (a different male on your arm, that is!) and you'd be foolish to dilute your fun by worring about being seen twice in the same dress. Think how unhappy you'd be if you had two formals—and only one invitation!

Q. *I'm a boy, sixteen, planning to go to my first formal dance at school. The word has gone out that the guys are supposed to wear tuxedos or dark blue suits, but I know most of the fellows are wearing tuxes. I don't own one and I can't afford to rent one (tickets and corsage will clean me out). I'd rather stay home than look conspicuous in a blue suit. How can I make my girl see my point of view?*

A. You can't, so don't even try. If you can't get an advance on your allowance to rent dinner clothes, then send your blue suit to the cleaners, dig out a dark bow tie from your father's collection—and off you go. There will undoubtedly be some other fellows in the same costume, and when the lights are low, who can tell what you're wearing, anyway?

Q. *The guys in my class seem to think I'm pretty square because I wear a shirt and tie and sport coat to school. Most of them wear shirts and sweaters with chinos. I'd do the same thing, except my mother has a big project going to improve the appearance of the whole faimly. She thinks we were all dressing too carelessly, and acting slopping as a result.*

I don't like the Little Lord Fauntleroy bit, but have you ever tried to deal with a determined mother?

A. It's true that sloppy dress can often lead to (or reflect) a sloppy frame of mind, so your mother has a point. But if you feel terribly out of place among your more casually dressed contemporaries, you'll be so self-conscious you won't be able to concentrate on school. See if you and your mother can't meet in neutral territory: chinos neatly ironed, a button-down shirt, open at the throat, and a sweater or sport coat. Nobody can argue with an outfit like that—not your mother *or* your buddy boys.

Q. *I have a problem which really confuses me. My mother works in the fashion department of a local store, and I know she has excellent clothes taste. She has always advised me on what to wear, and I think she's right about the kind of clothes which do the most for my type. My clothes are all very simple and understated and definitely chic. But now the prom is coming up. My mother has picked a marvelous dress, very simple, a copy of a Paris original. I know it's marvelous-looking, but all my friends are wearing bouffant things of lace and net and they'll think I look like a Cinderella. And I'm not sure what my fellow will think. I imagine he expects something fancy and frilly and loaded with sequins, and I don't want to disappoint him.*

A. If you know your prom dress is chic and right for you, don't let the expected opinions of your gal pals or your beau boy change your mind. You realize the frills and laces aren't your cup of tea, and you'd only feel uncomfortable in something that makes you look like every other girl on the dance floor. At least your date will be able to pick you out instantly from among all those moonlight-and-magnolia types.

Q. *Last month at a sale I bought a black leather jacket. This was very cheap and had a warm pile lining and, since I have to buy my own clothes, the price was important. Now my parents and my girl friend tell me I look like a hoodlum. I gave my old jacket away, so I'm stuck with this until I can save up enough for a replacement. Do clothes really make a man?*

A. Didn't you look in the mirror before you bought the jacket? Now that you're stuck with it, make sure you keep your hair cut short, your grooming impeccable and your behavior beyond reproach. And get a Saturday job to finance a new jacket. Clothes don't really make the man. But if you look like a Wild One, you can expect people to wonder if you really are.

Q. *My buddies say I'm not just a square, I'm a three-dimensional cube. O.K., maybe I am. But I'm red to the ears with embarrassment over my girl friend's bathing suit. She bought herself one of those itsy-bitsy bikinis, and she is definitely not stacked for it. She bulges in all the wrong places. I don't think she's ever looked at herself in a mirror. At the beach, I pretend she's not with me. How can I wise her up?*

A. Give your girl a beach robe—and a meaningful look. If she doesn't take the hint, suggest a glance in a full-length mirror. A three-way view of herself is usually enough to make any girl over twelve and more than two pounds overweight discard a bikini for a more conservative, flattering swimsuit.

Q. *Should a high-school girl wear gloves? My mother says no lady should be without them on important occasions. But I feel overdressed with them, except for church.*

A. If you're dressed up enough to wear high heels, you shouldn't be caught bare-handed. For downtown movie dates, going out for dinner, dances and dressy parties, you're not really completely groomed without gloves, either carried or worn. Hard as it may be for a teen to admit, mothers *do* know best now and then!

Q. *I wish you could give me some advice. The girl I go with wears Bermuda shorts on almost every date in summer. It seems to be the custom in her crowd, but I hate it. They're all right for picnics and sport dates, but when I take my girl to a movie, I want to feel I'm out with a real girl. How can I make her realize that guys like their dates to look feminine at least some of the time?*

A. Try commenting on how attractive other girls look in their swirly dresses. Let an appreciative eye linger a little longer than necessary on really feminine females as they pass. Bet on the next date your girl will be wearing a frothy dress, too, complete with high heels and perfume behind her ears!

Q. *My steady gave me a good-looking sweater for my birthday and then bought a matching one for himself. I hate to let him know that it bugs me to have us dressed alike. We're steadies, not Siamese twins. How can I tell him?*

A. Try a few kind words. Make it clear that, much as you love his gift, it embarrasses you to dress up and play house at your age. Then hope he understands. If he really likes you, at least he'll try.

Q. *Do you think a girl should go everywhere barefoot in the summer? My girl hates shoes, and she loves to shuck her sneakers on picnics, at the beach, for drive-in movies—just*

*about everywhere she can get away with being seen without
shoes. So far this summer, I've only seen her shod at church
and shopping on Main Street. She even went barefoot to
the country club dance, though I must admit I wouldn't
have known if I hadn't stepped on her toes! I think she's a
little nutty.*

A. Your gal is carrying the Nature Girl bit too far. Casual
comfort is O.K. on the beach or on picnics, but anything
more formal than that requires footwear. Drop a hint—but
watch out for those bare toes!

Q. *My mother doesn't approve of my going downtown
shopping wearing Bermuda shorts. All the girls do it, and I
don't know why I should be different. I'm always well-
groomed, and I'm built to wear shorts—so why should she
object?*

A. Even though Bermuda shorts are widely accepted
attire for many occasions, your mother is right—they aren't
really proper for in-town shopping, no matter how many
of your teen-aged friends think they are. You can be just
as cool and much more feminine in a flattering summer
dress. It's an advantage to remind yourself—and any sus-
ceptible males around—that you're a girl, and glad of it.

Q. *I never know what to wear to a party. Get-togethers
in our crowd range from very casual record-and-dance
parties to much dressier buffet suppers. But the hostess
never gives you much of a clue as to what's going on or
what you ought to wear.*

A. Speak right up and ask the hostess how formal the
party is going to be—or what she plans to wear, and take
your cue from that. Just be careful not to outshine the

hostess. It's bad manners and even worse strategy, if you want to be invited back again.

Q. *The principal of our school is concerned over the appearance of the students. It's his theory that sloppy appearance leads to sloppy behavior and slovenly mental attitudes. He has suggested that the student council, of which I'm president, issue a list of the ten best-dressed fellows and girls, to encourage everyone to spruce up. I know who'd get on it: the kids with the rich parents and big fat clothes allowances. I think those of us who scrape by would resent the list and it would do more harm than good.*

A. "Best-dressed" implies an expenditure of time and money which most high-schoolers can't afford. Perhaps you could award recognition to the "best-groomed" instead. Then everyone would have an equal chance to win, and there'd still be a spruced-up student body as a result. Makes more sense.

5 : *Date Planning*

"What'll We Do . . .?"

Q. *When I have guests over in the evening, my whole family sits around the living room like an audience, hanging on every word my friends and I say. I don't mind so much when it's a hen party, but when a boy friend comes over (I'm fifteen and not allowed to date yet, though my mother lets me have boys visit for the evening), it's a real drag. Can't my folks understand that we'd like a little privacy once in a while?*

A. That's a living room you're entertaining in, old dear, and you'll just have to pardon the rest of the family for living, too! You can't expect everyone to take cover the minute one of your friends rings the doorbell. Several solutions (or partial ones) come to mind. You could save your baby-sitting money and convert your room into a bed-sitting room, with couch instead of bed, a record player and maybe even a portable TV set, and do your entertaining there. Or you and your fellow friend can retreat to the kitchen, with the excuse you're going to make fudge or popcorn, and you can be alone with the appliances. Finally, you can just put up with the inconvenience of living five or six to a home, and bide your time till your sixteenth birthday and date-time privacy away from home.

Q. *I'm so sick of the movie-and-malted date bit I could scream. And yet when I ask a girl what she'd like to do when we go out, she never has anything more interesting to suggest. Don't girls want to do anything but sit and neck in a dark theater?*

A. Your date mates are probably screaming with boredom at the same old routine, too. But they hesitate to suggest anything else because they don't know the state of your wallet or your mind. It's up to the fellow to make the suggestions for fun plans. Next time, try ice skating in the park, a jazz concert, a Saturday afternoon wander through a museum, dinner at a foreign restaurant, even a walk through an unfamiliar part of town. Girls are dying to do something other than neck in the dark—just ask them!

Q. *A very special fellow seems to like me. At least, he comes over two or three times a week, and phones me every day. But he has never asked me for a real date or taken me anywhere. He's sixteen and has dated other girls, so it isn't that he's too shy. Also, he works part-time and I know he can afford to date. How can I make him realize that, though I like to have him come to my house, I want to go out occasionally, too?*

A. Why should the boy bestir himself and spend money when you seem perfectly happy with the current arrangement? Make a few discontented noises, and he'll come up with an honest date offer in a hurry. Better still, accept

other date offers. When the competition gets hotter, so will his interest in you.

Q. *Some of my buddies and I were chewing the fat the other night and we all came up with the same complaint. The girls never have any suggestions on what to do on date nights. I don't think guys should have to ask for the date, plan it and pay for it. Can't girls come up with a bright idea now and then?*

A. Next time you phone to make a date bid, say, "I'd like to take you out Friday night. I've got ten dollars (or whatever the sum in your jeans is) to blow. What would you like to do?" Then stand back! The suggestions will come so thick and fast you may wish you'd never asked!

Q. *Four weeks in a row now I've asked a certain girl for a date, and four times she's turned me down. The last time she didn't even bother to make up a good excuse. I really want to date her. How can I make her go out with me?*

A. Try to find out what sort of evening would make the girl really flip, then extend one more invitation, outlining the plans. If she still says "No," she just plain isn't on your wavelength and you can spend the evening in front of the mirror, making faces like a graceful loser!

Q. *About two weeks ago I sent a letter to a boy at college, inviting him to be my escort at our senior prom. I've never dated him, though I've had a crush on him for years and I thought this would be a good chance to get to know him. I haven't heard from him. Should I write again?*

A. The fellow may be too busy to write, but more likely he's too embarrassed. An invitation out of the blue from a girl he hardly knows, to as important an event as a prom, would embarrass the most stalwart character. If you haven't heard one word from him by now, you aren't likely to. Pick yourself another partner—someone you really know, this time. You need a date, not a test pilot!

Q. *The boy I'm going with doesn't have much money to spare, and I like to invite him home after a movie for a snack, instead of putting him to the expense of taking me out. The only trouble is that he doesn't seem to know when to go home. He hangs around so long that my parents get cross (at me!) and twice my father has come downstairs in robe and slippers, supposedly to raid the icebox, but really to send the fellow on his way. How can I make him realize the party's over?*

A. Every household has its rules, and it's only fair to outline those rules to your guest. Simply tell the boy, next time you issue an invitation, "My parents don't like me to entertain people after eleven-thirty (or whatever the witching hour happens to be)." He'll understand you're only being a dutiful daughter and not trying to unload him, so his feelings can't possibly be bruised. From then on, you shouldn't have any problems.

Q. *The other night I had my first date with a very nice boy, and he took me to a foreign restaurant for dinner. Obviously, he considered this a big treat, and I didn't have the heart to tell him I'm a picky eater. To make it worse, he ordered for me (he's something of an expert on food, it turns out) and kept urging me to try everything on my plate. I made the excuse that I had a headache, and barely nibbled. How can I keep from getting into such a pickle again?*

A. Too many girls go into a state of silent shock on dates. If a boy suggests a date plan that doesn't appeal to you, speak up and say so. That saves discomfort on your part and embarrassment to the boy when he realizes, as he will, that you're not having a good time. For dates to be fun, the evening's entertainment should be something you both enjoy. An obvious point, but too often one or the other date mate forgets it.

Q. *When a boy I've rarely dated asked me to a movie last weekend, he said, "Let's have dinner first." I got dressed up, thinking we were going to a fancy restaurant, and was surprised when he arrived in sport shirt and slacks. I was even more surprised, and insulted, when he took me to a drive-in 15¢ hamburger joint for "dinner." I never even got out of the car. Was I right to be mad?*

A. The next time the fellow invites you for dinner, ask him where. There's nothing wrong with his planning a cheap date (a boy's expenses are constant and high). But you can save yourself disappointment if you know ahead of time where you're going and can dress the part.

Q. *What can you do if a fellow refuses to get you home from a date on time? I have strict parents, and they're furious if I'm even ten minutes late. But when I try to nudge my guy toward the car during a party, he dawdles. I hate to be a drag by insisting and nagging.*

A. Let him get the word from on high. Before you leave on your next date, have your dad request, in his best Life with Father tones, that your fellow get you home at a certain witching hour. He'll be watching the clock all evening long!

Q. *My boy friend and I like different kinds of movies, and every Friday night there's a hassle about which show we'll see. I'm mad for foreign films and he's a fiend for shoot-'em-ups. How can we resolve this? Otherwise we get along very well.*

A. Try a month of your choosing the movie one Friday and his making the selection the next week. If you discover you really can't stand each other's film taste, then switch to other date activities and do your movie-going on your own time.

Q. *Last summer our crowd of fellows and girls went on many beach picnics, planned on the spur of the moment. At the end of the summer, we girls realized that the fellows always said, "You bring the food and we'll bring the drinks and ice." So we girls ended up supplying the hamburgers and hot dogs and rolls and pickles and mustard and watermelon, while the boys got by with a case of Cokes and a bag of ice cubes. We don't want to get stuck this way again. How can we avoid it?*

A. Next time a picnic is suggested, tell the fellows that, since men are the world's greatest cooks, they can bring the food this time. And from then on, alternate in providing the munching goodies. Turn about is fair play—and fair *pay!*

Q. *Whenever I call a certain girl for a date, she'll never say "Yes" until I tell her what the plans for the evening are. This irritates me because it sounds suspiciously like gold-digging. If she's interested in going out with me, why does she have to know what we're going to do?*

A. Most girls have to follow family rules about where they may go on date nights. Perhaps this is the reason why this girl grills you before accepting your date offers. It's less embarrassing to check first on the plans than to say "Yes" and then have to weasle out because you decide to take her to Joe's Place—and Joe's Place is off-limits for her.

Q. *My girl never seems to like the date plans I've made. If I suggest a movie, she says, "Let's go bowling instead." If I want pizza after a party, she votes for a steak. As often as not, what she suggests costs more than what I'd planned. How can I cope with this?*

A. Why not take turns making date plans? Every second time you invite the girl out, ask how she'd like to spend the evening. If you can afford her choice, you'll have the extra pleasure of knowing you're pleasing her.

". . . and with Whom?"

Q. *I'm a healthy specimen of American male, seventeen years old, five foot ten inches, reasonably attractive to females. My best buddy is very like me, only a little bit better in every way. He's taller, smarter, better at sports, good at small-talk, definitely more handsome, and absolutely irresistible to women—or at least to the women I'm interested in! Every time I find myself a new date mate and fall for her, I lose her to my buddy. He doesn't do it on purpose; girls just seem to flock around him. I can almost predict what will happen on a double date. My girl will start out interested in me, my buddy will hardly say a word to her, but at the end of the evening, the gal couldn't care less about me and is paying complete attention to my friend. I'm sick of being the loser, and I can't help resenting my buddy.*

A. You're not married to your buddy, and you're not Siamese twins. When you know he has a fatal attraction for females, you're only asking for trouble by planning double dates with him. Next time you have an attractive girl in your sights, become a loner. Arrange single dates until you're sure she's securely interested in you. Then (and perhaps not even then!) it's safe to introduce her to your fellow friend. Happy hunting—but don't allow any poaching. And why not send a picture of your buddy off to a Hollywood studio? If he's that spectacular, he's wasting his time hanging around the old home town!

Q. *My cousin has come from out-of-state to spend a month with us this summer. She is the same age as I, sixteen, and really quite a nice girl, but she doesn't seem to know how to get along with boys. I've arranged at least four dates for her, and not once has the fellow asked for a return engagement. My mother says I'm obligated to provide her with a date whenever I go out; I think I've done enough.*

A. You should include your cousin in group activities— parties, picnics, etc.—where she doesn't necessarily have to be paired off to have a good time. But when it's solo date night, you aren't obligated to make it a foursome. She was invited for a visit, not a crash course at charm school. You can't remake her personality in one month. Do everything you conveniently can to make sure she has a good time, but then relax and have fun on your own. Her personality problems are something she has to fix herself.

Q. *For about two months now I've been trying to get a date with a girl in my class. She's pretty and she's popular, and I've sure got eyes for her. But every time I ask her out, she says "No." It's true that she always has good excuses and really sounds sorry, and she's very friendly in school every day. But I can't help wondering if she likes me at all.*

A. If the girl is as pretty and popular as you suggest, it's not surprising that she has trouble juggling her date plans. Give her one more chance. Plan something at least two weeks off, an event that she'll find hard to resist, and one which requires tickets (it's a good excuse for asking her so far ahead). Then make one more date offer. If she finds you fun, she'll make an effort to wedge you into her crowded schedule from then on.

Q. *There's a slightly sensational girl in my class at school, very pretty and very popular. I've never dated much; in fact, it's only since I noticed this girl that I've ever had the inclination to pay attention to any female. I'd like to ask her out, but I can't think of any date activity that would intrigue her. She must get at least six date offers a week.*

A. If you decided to play professional baseball, you wouldn't aim immediately for the big leagues. And if mountain climbing were your hobby, Everest wouldn't be the first peak on your list of heights to conquer. So why expect to make the big time in date life, without a little practice? Put in some groundwork, walking-around work, with some of the less high-powered girls in your class before taking on the tops. Practice makes a perfect date—and you need lots of practice.

Q. *About a month ago I broke up with the boy I've been dating for six months. This leaves me without a date for our prom, and no time to find one. My mother has suggested I invite my cousin from out of town to be my escort. He's a* year older than I, very handsome, and I've always had a good time with him. But I'd be mortified if anyone found out he was my cousin. I'd almost rather stay home.

A. Import that cousin, and make him a man of mystery. He's attractive and fun, which will be enough to blind the girls at the dance. If anyone asks questions, just mention his name and say vaguely he's from out of town and you've "known him for years." You needn't deny he's a relative; just don't mention it. And be glad you have such a date, tailor-made for the emergency. Many girls aren't so lucky!

Q. *My boy friend and I often double with his sister and her beau, and the combination is driving me wild. The sister can't help monopolizing a conversation and I never feel I'm able to get a word in. I'm tired of being the silent member of the group, but I don't know how to change things. How do you tell a guy his sister is a big fat bore?*

A. Subtly suggest a change of double date partners, with a comment like: "Jane and Joe want us to go bowling with them Friday—it sounds like fun. I think I'd like the change." After a few such evenings, your fellow friend may notice you sparkle more when away from the competition of his chattery sister, and take the hint. If not, take fair warning. If the girl doesn't make a good double-date combination, she'll make a terrible sister-in-law!

Q. *It's been a hot summer in our town and the only place to go for relief is the air-conditioned movie. In the past couple of weeks, when my date comes to pick me up, my mother says, "If you'll wait a minute, I think Susie (my twelve-year-old sister) and I will ride along to the theater with you." This means my guy gets stuck with paying for*

*the tickets and we all have to sit together. I hardly ever get
a chance to see my guy anymore. He's very patient and good-
natured, but I know he's about fed up. How can I change
things?*

A. Next time this happens, drop your mother and sister
in front of the theater and go with your date to park his
car, announcing cheerily, "See you at home later." This
should be all the hint your mother needs to realize that the
family is intruding on your date life. It's *your* family, *your*
problem. It's up to you to resolve the awkward situation
before your guy departs the scene.

Q. *My girl is getting her diploma the second week in
June, and she has invited me to the graduation ceremony
and out to celebrate with her parents afterward. I like her
lots (though we're not steadies) and would like to share the
big night with her. But I'm scared of being tagged as her
private property if I accept the invitation to join the family
festivities, though I would like to attend the ceremony itself.*

A. Tell your girl that you'd like to watch her pick up her
diploma, but that you don't want to intrude on the family
gala afterward. Invite her instead to go out for a special date
the following night. She'll probably prefer your plans for a
"just us two" evening.

Q. *My parents are only in their late thirties and are pretty
gay social butterflies. Often, when I have a date, they suggest
that my guy and I join them for dinner. They're fun to be
with and everything, and I know that they're just trying to
get to know the boys I go out with. But you can understand
that being with my parents sort of cramps my style. No
matter how much a girl likes her parents, she really can't*

*feel completely relaxed with them on a date. I don't know
how to wiggle out of the invitations.*

A. Plot your date life a little more carefully, ringing in
another couple or firm plans for a party or a movie or a
bowling match. Then you can truthfully say, "Thanks, but
no, thanks," to your parents' offer to double-date on a two-
generation basis. Whenever you begin dating a new guy,
however, let your parents have a thorough look-see over
dinner. Your new beau shouldn't mind the scrutiny just once,
and he may welcome having the check picked up!

Q. *The boy I go with has a very close friend who always
double-dates with us. I like the boy and the girl he dates and
we always have a good time. But now and then I'd like to
go out with my date alone. How can I suggest this without
seeming either to chase him or brush off his friend?*

A. Why not say simply, "Why don't you and I go out, just
the two of us, sometime soon?" Your fellow will be flattered
and enjoy the mild pursuit.

Q. *The most wonderful thing in my life has happened.
A very special boy has invited me to a very special dance.
I was in the clouds until my mother told me I couldn't go
unless I got a date for my cousin, who is visiting us. It's a
"members only" dance at the country club, and I just can't
ask a fellow to provide a date for my cousin (who is quite
homely) and go to all that trouble and expense. It would
be different if I'd dated the boy before, but I haven't.*

A. Talk things over with your mother, calmly. Explain
the situation to her and make it clear that you'll have to
turn down the dance bid if your new-found fellow is re-

quired to act as a date bureau. Your mother should certainly understand your predicament, and can arrange to provide some other entertainment for your cousin that night to keep her from feeling too left out. Your big evening shouldn't be spoiled because of a house guest. The obligations for being a good hostess don't extend that far.

6 : *Entertaining*

Party Plans, Party Problems

Q. *I want to have a party on my sixteenth birthday next month. My parents have agreed to let me invite six boys and five girls for my first real boy-girl party. My folks are sort of old-fashioned, and they insist on hanging around as chaperones. I know this will put a damper on the whole thing. Why can't they go out to the movies like all the other parents do on party nights?*

A. Chaperones are as essential to teen-age parties as potato chips and ice cubes. Often high spirits need the restraining presence of adults to keep the kids from getting out of hand, swinging on the chandeliers and regretting it later. Your parents shouldn't stand guard in the party room, but they should wander through occasionally during the evening. If your folks are tactful, your guests will actually have a better time, knowing that they're having fun within the bounds of good behavior.

Q. *The boy I date has a large collection of "talk" records, discs made by Bob Newhart, Shelley Berman, Mort Sahl and others. Every time we spend an evening at his house, he insists on playing one or two of the records on his big new hi-fi set, and everyone has to sit still as mice and listen. This knocks out the converstation. How can I make him understand that the hi-fi should provide "background" at parties, not take over completely?*

A. Your guy is shy and uncertain of being able to make interesting conversation on his own, and so calls out the recorded reserves. Next time your record buff makes a move for the record pile, take him aside and tell him, "I don't care how many speakers your hi-fi has; *you're* the one I want to hear." Then listen!

Q. *My mother loves to give parties. Whenever I mention that I'd like to have a few kids over, her eyes light up and she begins thumbing through her collection of recipes. As a result, I always have the most elaborate parties in my crowd, and it embarrasses me. What I really want is a casual affair, with Cokes and potato chips and dancing to records. How can I make her understand?*

A. Tell your mother as tactfully as possible (don't insult the cook, or you'll be sorry every dinner hour for weeks) that you feel conspicuous by giving such fancy parties. Let her know that Cokes and chips are standard fare in your crowd, and much easier on the budget. That last item should be the clincher!

Q. *Are games just too corny for high-school parties? Usually at our shindigs the boys gather at one end of the room and the girls congregate at the other side and no one has much fun. But if the hostess suggests games, loud moans go up from both corners.*

A. Since nobody seems to be having a divine time anyway, games can't help but improve the situation. Ignore the moans, recruit one or two friends to help you get things organized and begin the games. Games like charades, Inky Pinky ("What's an overweight feline?"—"A fat cat!") and Ghosts can get a dragging party off the ground. And you may be surprised to discover that those who moan loudest about the games are the ones who end up as the most enthusiastic players.

Q. *Whenever I give a party, the guests always stay too long. I guess I should be flattered that they're having such a good time they don't want to leave, but my parents get steamed at the late hours. How can I let my friends know when it's time to go home?*

A. First of all, make the party deadline explicit in your invitation. "Won't you come to a party, eight to twelve on Friday night?" Then enlist the help of one or two girl friends. Explain your problem, and ask that they start the homeward movement about fifteen minutes before deadline. Most guests will drift off, once the party begins to break up, but diehards may need an extra nudge. If your yawning, collecting dishes and gathering up glasses doesn't give them the hint, just say, "I'm sorry to have to call it an evening, but my parents don't like me to have people stay past midnight." It's true, and what's even better, it works!

Q. *My seventeenth birthday is in two weeks, and my mother wants to give me a boy-girl party. I like the idea, but I don't want my guests to feel they have to bring a present. Would it be all right to issue the invitations without mentioning that it's my birthday? Or will the guests feel em-*

barrassed when a lighted birthday cake is brought out at dessert time?

A. Do the cake and candle bit with your family either before the guests arrive or on another "substitute birthday" day. Then you won't make your guests uncomfortable about not having brought presents. If the news should leak out that it's your birthday, tell your friends that *they* are what you wanted most for a present—and got!

Q. *Whenever I give a party, the evening is spoiled for me because there's such a mess to clean up afterward. All the guests drift off and leave me to stack the dishes, put away Coke bottles, vaccum up crunched potato chips and file the records. My mother insists that the clean-up detail is my responsibility, but it sure takes the fun out of party-giving.*

A. O.K., so you're litter-bugged. Next time you give a party, invite one of the guests to spend the night with you afterward. Before you hit the sack, the two of you can police the area, rehashing the party as you work. You'll halve the labor and double the fun.

Q. *I'm fourteen and just beginning to give boy-girl parties. No matter how carefully I plan things (refreshments and games and dancing), sometime during the evening someone suggests we play kissing games. Before I know it, the lights are out and everybody is squealing and giggling and the party has fallen apart. Last week I barely got the lights on and the boys barely got the lipstick off their faces before my parents returned from the movies.*

A. When a fourteen-year-old entertains, her parents should be on the spot, not off at the movies. You don't have to refer to your folks as "chaperones," just as long as they're around to wander through now and then. You'd be surprised how the lights stay on when there's someone over twenty-one in the house!

Q. *I've been invited to a masquerade party. Frankly, I don't have the time or the money to dream up a special costume. But all my friends are going and I don't want to be left out.*

A. Enter imagination! Any leopard printed towels in your mother's linen closet? Two of them, sewed up the side edges, leaving room for armholes, and anchored at the shoulder, make you into a cave dweller. The illusion is completed by a bone from the butcher, scrubbed clean and tied in your hair (for girls) or brandished menacingly in the direction of any lurking saber-toothed tigers (for boys). You can turn yourself into a Emmett Kelly-type clown in one of your father's old suits and battered fedoras, with lipsticked nose and burnt cork-blackened eyes. Or how about a hoodlum out of the 20's (pin-striped suit, dark shirt, light tie, hat pulled down over your eyes, cigarette dangling from the corner of your mouth)? Or a beatnik? Or a Charles Addams cartoon character? Most of these disguises can be put together with a small amount of effort and a large dash of creativity from things to be found at home in closets or attics. So accept that invitation and get to work—you'll be late for the party!

Q. *Now that I'm sixteen, I'm beginning to give parties about once a month. I wonder if a party for teen-agers should have decorations. I know we're too old for crepe paper streamers and balloons hung from the ceiling, but I think something should be done to make the rooms look festive and exciting.*

A. The best decorations you can provide are an attractive group of fellows and girls obviously having fun. But now and then, you might give a special motif party to jazz up the social schedule. Ask guests to come to a Bon Voyage party and hang travel posters on the walls to give them something extra to look at and talk about. Or putting red-checked tableclothes on card tables centered with candles stuck in empty bottles makes something special out of an ordinary pizza party. Card tables ranged along the edges of the room, each covered with a white cloth and decked out with a candle and a single rose in a bud vase, can quickly turn your living room into an "night club." When you have the extra time and cash for such pre-party preparations, the investment pays off in extra fun and gives you a reputation for being an imaginative hostess.

Q. *I've been trying to catch up on back entertaining and am having four couples over every Friday night to pay back my obligations. I have a friend who is very sensitive. She acts hurt if she isn't invited to every single party. I don't want to upset her.*

A. Stop feeling so guilty. Simply tell the girl you're paying off your social debts by having a few people in at a time for a series of parties. She won't feel left out if she knows she wasn't left off the guest list for a big party. Clue her in.

Q. *I'm planning to give a party, my first boy-girl entertaining. I rarely date and don't want to be stranded at my own party without an escort. Yet I don't know how to invite a boy so that he'll realize he's supposed to be my date. Can you help me?*

A. Invite the boy you like, saying quite clearly, "I'm giving a party on Friday and I'd like you to come as my date." That way, there can be no misunderstanding and the fellow can accept or decline on that basis.

Q. *A group of us girls (we're fourteen-year-olds) got together and gave a party last weekend. We paid for everything and invited a crowd of boys from school. They were just awful. They clowned around, didn't dance with any of the girls, and went home as soon as the food was gone. Do you think we should try again?*

A. Give the fellows another chance. At fourteen, they're not nearly as socially mature as you gals, nor are they so eager to polish off the rough edges. Next time, plan a more active party: a hayride, a picnic on a Saturday afternoon or an evening party with organized games and tag dances. Those fourteen-year-old wild ones are going to need a little taming—and you're just the girls who can crack the whip.

Q. *In our town, there's a group of six or eight boys who think it's hilarious to gate-crash. Every party our crowd gives is spoiled by having these fellows show up uninvited. They're nice enough fellows, I guess, except that they can't stand to be left out of things—so they crash. I'm having a party next weekend, and don't want it ruined. How can I prevent their breaking in?*

A. Let your father do the greeting chores at the front door on the big night. It's easier to keep uninvited guests out than to ask them to leave, once they've crashed. And your father, with his adult authority, will be more effective than you could ever be. For future parties, you might consider adding these fellows to the guest list, since you don't seem to have anything against them except their gate-crashing tactics. If you can't lick 'em—ask 'em to join you!

Q. *Even when the music is good and the lights are low, the boys don't ask the girls to dance at our parties. Some of the girls, out of desperation, dance with each other. Do you think this is a good idea?*

A. If a fellow hasn't the courage to walk up to *one* girl and ask her to dance, how's he going to muster the nerve to cut in on *two?* Go ahead and dance with a female partner, *if* you want to dance with girls all evening long. But if you want to lure the fellows out on the floor, ask one or two boys (friend types, rather than date types) to get things started, and use tag dances and girl-asks-boy sets to keep things going. Too embarrassed to invite a boy to dance, you say? Aren't you even more embarrassed to sit on the sidelines all evening long, waiting for the party to come alive?

Q. *I'm having a party for my sixteenth birthday and the whole evening can be perfect, if—I've got the friends, the records, a date for myself and my parents' permission, but we can't afford to spend more than ten dollars (my baby-sitting savings) on refreshments. What can I serve that will look like a party and still get twelve hungry teen-agers satisfied?*

A. If the party mood is right, any food tastes good, and this simple menu will taste wonderful: home-made chili, rye bread and butter, dill pickle slices and doughnuts with fruit punch. (Check a good recipe book for a tea-based punch made with fruit; serve it cold and fruit-trimmed, add ginger ale.) You'll have more than enough food, with change left over from that ten-dollar bill. Keep a couple of extra cans of kidney beans handy, in case that chili pot gets low when guests are asking for *fourths.*

Q. *Whenever I give a party, the boys (fourteen and fifteen) end up by watching television. I know they're shy and don't really like parties much, but I think they'd have a better time if they didn't just sit and stare at the set. What can I do?*

A. If the set isn't portable enough to move out of the party room for the evening, then pull the plug and announce that the TV isn't working tonight. As long as you don't have a do-it-yourself Mr. Fixit in the crowd, your fellow friends should turn their attention to the main attraction: you and your gal pals.

Q. *When I'm hostess at a party with guests who don't know each other, I never know how to make sure everyone meets everyone else. Do I have to take each new arrival around the room and introduce her to every single person?*

A. At a small party (ten guests or less) you ought to make the rounds, trying to wind up by introducing the new arrival to the guest you think is most likely to enjoy the newcomer. At bigger parties, however, present a guest to a single group, trying to pick a cluster of people who either share an interest of the arrival, or who are relaxed and friendly enough to put a stranger at ease. When the party is large, each guest has an obligation to introduce himself to others, without following the hostess around like a stray puppy. It's up to the guests to help make the party go. The hostess has provided the place, the people, the refreshments, the music. She can't do everything!

Q. *I gave a party the other night and noticed that all the guys were sneaking out and coming back acting sort of silly. It never occurred to me that they were drinking, but I learned later that one of the guys brought a pint in the glove compartment of his car, and everyone was slipping out for a sip. The party was ruined (the boys wouldn't dance with the girls or talk to them; they just stood around snickering at having put one over on us) and I'm mad. What should I have done? The boys are fifteen and sixteen.*

A. This is a problem for your parents to handle. You should have alerted your father, who could have confiscated the liquor, spoken sharply to the culprits and sent the pint-toter home. Adults aren't around only to chaperon at teen parties; they come in very handy to take over in situations you can't handle yourself. Keep this in mind for the next crisis.

Q. *My girl friend lives in a small apartment with no room to give a party. She suggested that we co-hostess a party at my house and split the expenses. I think she should pay for at least two-thirds of the food. After all, it's my house.*

A. Hey, there! Is this a friendship or a business partnership? If you like the girl well enough to sponsor a party with her, then don't quibble over the expenses. Split them right down the middle—or risk doing the same to the friendship!

Q. *Ever since I was a little girl my mother has planned marvelous parties with pretty decorations, good games and prizes for everyone. Now I'm having a boy-girl party for my fifteenth birthday and Mother is organizing everything again. She's planning to use paper plates, paper cups and a paper tablecloth. I think we're old enough to have real silver and china and candles on the table. Mom says she doesn't*

*want the messy clean-up or the worry about her good china.
It's going to spoil the whole evening if it looks like a kids'
party. She'll probably expect us to play Pin the Tail on the
Donkey!*

A. You're right; your mother's wrong. Offer to take over
the clean-up chore and to replace anything that gets cracked,
nicked or broken. Then hope your mother will reconsider
and realize you're old enough now to be a gracious, and
careful, hostess. Paper hats and paper plates don't fit
fifteen-year-old plans.

Q. *I have two groups of close friends—the crowd from
school and a circle of fellows and girls from my church youth
group. I'd like them to get to know each other. I'm thinking
of giving one big bash and inviting everyone, about thirty
people in all. Do you think it would work?*

A. At that big a party, everyone is likely to stick with his
own crowd, and there won't be any mingling, defeating the
purpose of the party. Better to give two or three smaller
parties, mixing the groups, so that old friends don't cluster
together. It won't add up to much more in expenses, though
you'll have to reserve the living room three Friday nights
in a row and give your mother a solemn promise that you're
a one-girl clean-up crew.

Casual Entertaining

Q. *I'm fifteen, a high-school sophomore, and reasonably
popular. But my social life is being ruined because I can't
invite anyone over to our apartment in the evenings anymore. About six weeks ago, my father took a new and very
demanding job, and my mother has decided that I can't have
guests after he comes home in the evening, except on Fri-*

day nights, when they go out. I'm allowed to have kids stop in after school, but they have to move on before darling daddy gets home. I think my mother is pampering him terribly, and not paying enough attention to my needs. What do you think?

A. I think you're griping a little early in the game. Once your father becomes familiar with his new job and completes his shakedown period, home entertaining rules are likely to be relaxed again. Meantime, enjoy the after-school and Friday night guests, and do everything possible to make your dad's homecomings pleasant and relaxed. He'll appreciate the thoughtfulness. A man's home is supposed to be his castle. But when he has a pretty teen-aged daughter, it's often so cluttered up with knights on white horses that he can't get the peace he has earned!

Q. *My folks built a great recreation room in our base- ment, hoping that we kids would stay home, instead of roaming the streets. We stay home, all right—you can barely get out the front door through the crush of friends who are dying to use the pinball machine, Ping-Pong table, work- bench, etc. It's getting so I haven't time to do my home- work, read or just hack around on my own. How can I clear the gang out?*

A. Pass the word that it's "open house" at certain hours, two or three days a week; the rest is homework or family time. Make your friends welcome when they truly are, but don't let your hospitality be abused. You have to keep a corner of your life—and your home—for yourself.

Q. *Do I have to serve refreshments every time someone drops in for a visit? Sometimes my girl friends arrive to do homework with me, or a boy stops by just to say Hello when*

he's in the neighborhood. We have a large family and often we're fresh out of snacks. My mother howls when I dip into family food to feed my friends.

A. It's always polite and welcoming to offer some tidbit to guests who stay for more than fifteen minutes. But that snack could be as simple as a cup of coffee or a bowl of popcorn. Ham sandwiches, bottled soft drinks, crackers and cheese are a strain on the family food budget. But home-popped corn, fruit flavored punch, potato chips and such snacks can come out of your baby-sitting earnings and be squirreled away on a special shelf for your visitors. You'll keep your guests happy and your mother from tearing her hair in financial frustration.

Q. *I am a girl, fifteen, who has very strict and very popular parents. They will never let me entertain a boy, or a group of girls and boys, when they're not at home. And the trouble is that they're almost never at home! They go out at least four nights a week, including Friday and Saturday. As you can see, this gives me practically zero in my "social studies." I'm willing to abide by their no-date rule, but if they insist on a chaperone for at-home entertaining, I think that's where they should be—at home!*

A. Looks as if your parents are so dizzied by their own social whirl that they can't see your difficulties clearly. Try to catch your mother in a quiet moment and talk things over with her. Ask if you can set up a schedule so that you can entertain at least one weekend evening every two weeks. If your parents can't manage to be at home to supervise, suggest that your mother arrange for two friendly relatives to take over the chaperone chores. Better hurry and catch your busy mother—there she goes out the door now!

7 : *School*

Teacher Troubles

Q. *I'm in the clutches of a teacher who hates me. We've never gotten along, though I study hard and do very well in her classes. Unfortunately, she teaches courses I have to have for college entrance. I can't figure out why she dislikes me and picks on me all the time. I'm not exaggerating or imagining things, either; all my classmates notice the way she keeps hammering away at me. I'm afraid she'll give me a bad grade, and I need every A I can get to make the college I've chosen.*

A. Personality clashes are inevitable between some teachers and some students, no matter how hard each tries to get along with the other. Check your own behavior and attitudes to make sure you haven't done anything to irritate the teacher. If you emerge with a clear conscience, you'll just have to grin and bear it for the rest of the term. But take heart on two scores. If the teacher doesn't like you, she'll probably bend over backward to be fair when it's time to hand out grades, so her own conscience will be clear. And sometimes professors who are toughest to get along with and who hammer away at students are those who bring out the best effort in their classes. In extending your-self just to "show her," you may end up with much better grades than you'd have earned without the pressure.

Q. *I'm fourteen and have a terrific crush on my French teacher. I feel so awful, because I know I don't mean any-thing to him. He has a wife and two darling children, but I can't stop thinking about him. I'm getting worried.*

A. You can relax and stop worrying. Crushes on older and "unavailable" men are as common in adolescence as braces and bad complexions. It's all a perfectly normal part of turning from child into woman, so just ride out the storm. Be careful not to embarrass yourself by letting your crush become too obvious, either to the teacher or to your friends. Work hard in his class to win his approval—but realize you'll never win him. This time next month (or next year) all that affection will be directed toward someone your own age and available—possibly that attractive, crew-cut type who sits right in front of you in French class!

Q. *I've always been good at art and have a flair for caricature. Last week, during study hall, I sketched the principal and I'm afraid it wasn't very flattering. The study hall supervisor saw what I was doing and hauled me off to the principal's office, where I got a real dressing down. How can I get back in everyone's good graces? Or can I?*

A. This can't be the first time the principal has found him-self the target of a student's pointed pen, and he's probably used to it. He may even be secretly amused. A written apology should get you off the hook. Next time, be smart enough to exercise your art talent outside school hours. During study period, you're meant to study. Period.

Q. *The principal of our school has just issued a "dress right code" for the students, and I'm about to flip. The rules include no more jeans for boys, no slacks for girls during class hours. I have always found jeans the most economical way to dress, and because I have to earn my own clothes money, this is important to me. I'm always clean and well-groomed and my jeans fit well, not low-slung and tight like some guys wear. Do you think there's any point in protesting the new rules? Nobody else seems too mad.*

A. Many high-school principals have discovered that raising the standards of dress in their schools also raises the standards of behavior. When attitudes toward clothing are too casual, so are the attitudes toward rules. It doesn't look as if your lone voice of protest would do much good, so dig into the sock and buy yourself some chinos. And don't sulk. If you had an office job, you couldn't come to work in levis, either!

Q. *I bought a small Christmas present for a favorite teacher and then discovered that the class was taking up a collection to buy a group gift. I'd still like to give the teacher my individual present, though I also contributed to the class gift. Do you think it would look too much like apple polishing?*

A. No reason why you shouldn't say, "Thank you for a good year" with your own present, as long as you don't think you're swapping this extra thoughtfulness for a higher grade. You know that teachers work hard for too little money.

Christmas is a good chance to extend the thanks that make their sacrifices seem worthwhile.

Q. *I have a rather odd question, but I'd like your opinion. I'm fifteen, and have a very good English teacher, male. The other day in class he said to me, very abruptly, "You're wearing too much lipstick, Judy." I was startled and annoyed. I didn't think it was any of his business. I don't wear much lipstick and what I do wear, I wear with my mother's advice and approval. I told him I wouldn't wear so much to his class if he objected, and dropped the subject. But I can't help wondering. Do you think he had any right to criticize my makeup? And should I defer to his opinion, as I said I would?*

A. Many teachers consider themselves educators, mentors and substitute parents. These types often make the most stimulating teachers, but they may also overstep their bounds now and then, either through a genuine concern for the pupil or because of a heady sense of power. Defer to this teacher's wishes if you like, this time. But if you ever fear his interest is more personal than professional, let your mother take the matter up with the principal or discuss it at the next PTA meeting.

Q. *I'm sixteen, approaching my junior year in high school and doing very well in my studies. I'm always on the honor roll, belong to the French Club and am fairly popular, though I don't find time to date too much. I'm quite satisfied with the way my high-school career is going, but two of my teachers think I don't participate in enough extracurricular activities to be "well-rounded." I think my energy and time should be directed to study. What do you think?*

A. With college entrance competition as tough as it is, top grades are of primary importance, of course. But many colleges are paying increasing attention to over-all high-school activity, and are interested in "leader types." If you can join another club or two to round out your activities, without sacrificing grades, it would be a wise plan of action.

Q. *I've switched to a new school this year where the teachers are very strict. Having come from a permissive school, where the teachers were more interested in content than form, I'm surprised (and angered) by getting bad grades on homework because of "untidiness" or bad penmanship. For instance, I got a C— on an English composition last week, though the teacher said it was the best writing he's had submitted in seventeen years of high-school teaching. The excuse for the mark: sloppy typing! He said he knew I was capable of much neater work. Who cares if a paper is neat, as long as the thoughts come from a well-ordered mind?*

A. You've found out the hard way: neatness counts! A well-ordered mind can't do its best within the framework of sloppy work habits. Neatening your homework papers will be valuable self-discipline. Even Shakespeare might have gone unnoticed if no one had been able to read his handwriting!

Q. *I'm a senior in high school and do modeling on the side, because I want to be either a model or an actress when I get out of school. I work hard, both in and out of school. I make a good income for a girl my age, and I get excellent grades. But there's one teacher who seems to think it's her mission in life to keep me from getting stuck up. She's al-*

ways needling me with such comments as "Has our career girl found time to do her assignment?" *or* "I expect this work to be completed by Friday. Do you think you can fit it into your busy schedule, Miss Model?" *I've never been late with an assignment all year! My mother says the teacher resents me because I'm attractive and the teacher is downright ugly. But that doesn't help me much.*

A. Your teacher is the one with the real problem. The only thing for you to do is to continue to work hard and pay as little attention as possible to her needling. Your difficulty will end at the close of the term. She's stuck with her ill temper and bitterness indefinitely. Of the two, you're the lucky one.

Q. *Our homeroom teacher is retiring at the end of the school year and the class would like to give her a special present. Do you have any bright ideas? There are thirty-two of us in the class, and we each plan to contribute at least one dollar. She's a great old gal, and we want her to remember her last class.*

A. Armed with $32 or more, you should be able to find a really memorable gift for Miss Chips. The present should be something lasting, as you realize. Check with one or two other teachers to see if she has expressed any desires. Perhaps she'd like to have something donated to the school in her name: a framed print of one of her favorite paintings to be hung in the school hall, a set of books for the library, some records to be added to the school collection. Or, for something she can wear with pride and happy memories, you might decide on a gold link bracelet, with a single gold disc attached. Have the circle engraved with her initials, the date of retirement, Class of 19— and whatever brief sentiment the class decides on.

Q. *I've always had a reputation for being a little boy-crazy and I guess I've deserved it. But I really think I'm slowing down a little. My new problem is that I'm having trouble in my English course and would like a little after-class help. But the teacher is a gorgeous hunk of stuff, and if I asked for his assistance, I know everyone would razz me and accuse me of being on the make. Truth is, even I wouldn't know whether my main interest is jacking up my grades or spending a little time alone with dreamboat.*

A. Make *one* after-class appointment with the prof, ask his advice on *independent* work to help raise your grades and then buckle down. You'll never improve your marks, even with after-hours tutoring, if you're mooning over the teacher instead of poring over the books.

Q. *There's a teacher in our school who is a real horror. Nothing any of us does pleases her. You can work your hide off on an assignment, and she's never satisfied. She's always telling us we're intellectually lazy and disorganized and pampered and trying to coast through high school. She's driving us all wild. To get an A in her course is practically impossible.*

A. Try a little experiment. Make a list of the five toughest and most demanding teachers you've had in your high-school career. Now make a list of the five courses in which you felt you learned the most, which you found the most stimulating and intellectually satisfying. I'll bet a cookie that at least three of those courses were taught by a teacher from your "tough list." Get the message?

Q. *None of my teachers seem to like me. They never ask me to help decorate the classroom or do any jobs for them;*

they only take their pets. I'm an average student and I don't think it's fair.

A. Most teachers find it hard to resist a student who shows an extra spurt of interest and enthusiasm. Even if you're an ordinary student, you can work extraordinarily hard—do extra assignments, ask extra-sensible questions in class, volunteer to help with class projects without waiting to be asked. Your teachers can't help but respond to your zest.

Q. *I turned in a book report the other day and got it marked F because the teacher said she didn't approve of the book I'd chosen. We were supposed to report on the book we enjoyed most in the last month and she didn't give us a reading list or anything. I thought it was a very good book, but maybe a little racy for this old-maid teacher.*

A. Did you really choose the book because you thought it was the best you'd read, or because you thought your choice might shake up your "old maid teacher"? Be honest. And then turn in another book report which you know will be acceptable. The teacher makes the rules; you'd better play by them.

Making the Grade

Q. *I'm going with a boy who is a real grind. He's very attractive and fun to be with, but he's so determined to get good grades that he'll only date once a week. And when he phones to chat during the evening, he'll talk for five minutes, then excuse himself to study. I'm tired of coming in second to a stack of books!*

A. This sounds like a boy who knows the facts of academic life. He's aware of how difficult it is to get into good colleges, and he's determined that nothing, not even the girl in his life, will interfere with his hauling down good grades. He knows if he doesn't hit the books, he'll hit the skids. If this is a boy you really care for, help him achieve his ambitions by leaving him free to study. And what will you do with the extra time this leaves you? You might try cracking the books harder yourself. He's going to want someone to talk to—and he won't want to use just one-syllable words!

Q. *I know that three guys in my class, friends of mine, are cheating on homework and on tests. I can hardly blame them, because both school and home pressure to get good grades is tremendous. But I work hard for my good marks, and I resent their slipping by so easily. I also worry about their getting caught. They'd be expelled for sure. What should I do?*

A. Tell the fellows you're on to their secret, and then give them the old pep talk: they're only cheating themselves, they'll ruin their academic careers if they're caught, they'll find college tough going if they don't learn to come by good grades honestly. Then cap it with the regretful announcement that you'll report them if they don't stop. They may be angry at you (nobody likes to be caught redhanded), but *someday* they'll be grateful. They won't say "Thanks" now, so you'll just have to keep yourself warm with the knowledge that you've done the right thing.

Q. *I'm going into my senior year in high school and plan to attend college next year. My grades are good enough so far, but I've really had to hit the books hot and heavy. I didn't have much fun last year, with only about two dates a month. This year I'm tempted to go lighter on the study, and have a little more fun. After all, it's my senior year and the last chance to pal around with the guys I've gone around with all through high school. I figure that if I flunk anything, I can take the course in summer school. Do you think this is a nutty idea?*

A. Face the facts: if you insist on having too gay a time during your senior year in high school, you won't have any fun at all during your freshman year at college—because you won't be admitted!

Q. For my birthday, my family gave me a little pink radio and I love it. But my parents object when I keep it on while I do my homework. My homework takes about three hours every school night so, unless I play it then, I'd never hear it. Don't you think this is unfair?

A. Only a genius could do two things well at the same time. And since your homework takes three hours, well—let's not argue about *that!* Try working in total silence and you'll probably have at least an hour to spare after homework for listening and relaxing.

Q. I want to quit school and go to work. My dad has been laid off from his job. I'm over sixteen and could be helping out. I can't stand to see my folks looking so worried all the time. But they make a big fuss if I even mention quitting. What good does it do anyone to have me waste time at school when the bills are piling up, my little sister needs her teeth fixed, and we're eating beans? My dad quit school after eighth grade and he didn't do so bad until lately.

A. As your dad will be the first to tell you, things have changed since he was young. Automation is taking over the unskilled jobs formerly filled by workers who didn't finish school. A high-school diploma is becoming more and more a necessity for landing a decent job. Without it, you'll find work only as a helper, loader, laborer or messenger, usually with nonprestige companies. There are fewer openings for non-graduates and what jobs there are, generally have lower salaries and less opportunity for advancement. You can't hope for more than $1.25 an hour, even if you're lucky enough to land a job at all. In one of the largest states in the nation, where a special section has been set up in the state employment department to secure work for "drop-outs" (those teens who don't stay on in school until graduation), jobs could be found for only one out of three job-seekers. Your family is going through a tough financial period, and it's commendable that you want to help. But don't sell out your future. Get part-time and Saturday work to help ease the current money problems, but stick to school at all costs. That's the biggest and most important "job" you have right now, even if you don't get "paid" until after graduation.

Q. *I'm a sophomore at a special high school in our city. The school is for "gifted" students and the average IQ is around 140. It's a great school, but we all take a lot of ribbing from kids who don't attend. "Oh, you're one of the brains" is the usual reaction when someone asks me where I go to school. I'm tired of having to explain that I'm just like other fifteen-year-olds, like to dance and date and have fun. Why should I have to apologize for my brains all the time?*

A. Don't *explain* that you're like other kids; just *act* like them. New friends won't mind the fact that you are superior so much as they'll resent your *acting* superior to them. Accept your extra ration of brains as you would any other fortunate cirucmstance, like curly hair or athletic ability. As long as you're neither smug nor defensive about your IQ, most people won't give it a second thought.

Q. *My guy is in trouble and I'd like to help him but I don't know how. He was caught cheating on a test and is now on probation. There was a reason for his cribbing, but he's too proud to explain it to the powers that be. His family has always counted on his going to college, but he'll have to win at least a partial scholarship to swing it. He has always studied hard and gotten good grades. Just before this important test, his mother was sick and he had to help take care of two younger brothers and didn't get time to study as usual. He was so worried about not making a good mark that he cheated. I know this doesn't excuse what he did (it was wrong and we both know it) but at least it explains his actions. Ours is a big school and the teachers can't possibly know about all the ins and outs of home life. I'm sure they'd be more lenient or at least more understanding if they knew the circumstances. But he won't talk to anyone.*

A. If you're sure your beau boy won't think you're intruding, ask to talk to his teacher. Explain that you've come on your own and the fellow would perhaps be annoyed if he knew. Without special pleading, tell the teacher you think she ought to know the background of the cheating. Lay the facts on the line, and leave the rest up to her. It may help. And even if it doesn't, you'll feel better for having tried.

Q. *I'm sixteen and a high-school sophomore. My dad says I watch TV far too much, that my eyes are going to bug out* *and my brains jell. He bought an encyclopedia and promised me $1,000 if I read all twenty-four volumes by the time I get out of high school. I think he's flipped his wig. But that $1,000 looks mighty good. It would buy a keen car.*

A. You'll never get $1,000 for watching TV, unless you luck into it on a quiz show. Take your father up on his offer. Ten years from now, you'll feel like paying him $10,000 for suggesting the reading program. And you'll be able to do it, too, out of the extra earnings your added knowledge made possible!

Q. *I don't dig school at all. Shakespeare and math and all that jazz don't get to me. I'm not stupid (so the teachers keep telling me—there's lots of yap about my "potential"), but I can't get with it. I want to get away from dusty books and get out into the world where things are really happening. Working in a garage or just hacking around would be better than being locked in a stuffy old school all day. I'm choking on chalk dust. But my old man says if I quit school, I'll have to find another place to live. That's O.K. with me. I don't call this living.*

A. Quit school now and you'll boot your future right out the window. Without that migic diploma, you'll find it tough to get any kind of job at all. Even if you find work (and only one-third of "drop-outs" do), it will be the kind that pays little and goes nowhere. If you're restless and dissatisfied now, you'll be in worse shape with no job to do, no place to go during the day, no friends except other "drop-outs." If you can't "get with it," it's probably because you haven't yet made the connection between what you're learning in school and what you need to know to make it in the world outside. The math you're knocking is useful in all but the lowest skilled (and lowest-paying) jobs. Maybe you'd do better in a combination vocational-academic course, where the link between what you learn from books and its practical application is quickly apparent. Or does your school offer a school-work program, where you can spend half your time in classes, half the time on a job, alternating with another working student? Can you find yourself after-school and Saturday work which will prove to you that what you learn in school isn't filed under F for Forget when you take a job? Quit school now and you won't be "getting out into the world"; you'll be resigning from it.

Q. *I'm very good in English and practically idiotic in math. My buddy is a mathematical genius, but can hardly put two words together. We're both hoping for college. He suggested that he'd do my math homework for me, if I'd write his English Lit. assignments for him. Together, we'd make a great team. I don't know whether I should take him up on his offer.*

A. Together, you'd certainly make a great team, but you can do it without cheating. Instead of doing each other's assignments, get together two or three nights a week to coach each other on your weak subjects so that you can haul up your grades legitimately. You can't drag him along to balance your checkbook for the rest of your life, or tag along after him to write his letters. Certainly, help each other, but do it in an honest, lasting way.

Q. *Man, the college pressure is on around our house! My folks are so worried about my getting good grades that they insist that I do my homework at a certain hour and in a certain place every night. It makes me so mad to be pushed* around (a sixteen-year-old guy should run his own life) that I dawdle and stall and don't get as much done as I could if they'd just leave me alone. When will they treat me like a grown-up?

A. Probably the minute you start acting like one! If you're so sure you can run your own life, then run it! Set aside a time and place for study yourself, and stick to your schedule. Your parents will stop nagging you the minute you no longer need nagging.

Q. Our English teacher is always telling us to write from our own experience. We were supposed to do a story with a romantic background, so I wrote about the first time I was ever kissed. Though I changed the names and the details, nevertheless many people recognized the boy, the first fellow I ever went steady with. The kids are teasing me like crazy, and the boy is so mad he won't even talk to me. Do I owe him an apology or anything? After all, I was just following the teacher's suggestion.

A. Next time you get the needle, you can say, "What makes you think the story is about Jim?" That'll set the crowd (and Jim) to wondering if they were so smart in their guessing game, after all—if you walk away quickly, while they're still pondering!

Q. I'm sort of an early bird. I like to get up at the crack of dawn, when the rest of the family is still asleep, and do my homework then. I'm fresh and full of bounce, and can whiz through it in double-time. But my mother nags every night when I sit around and watch TV or read; it bugs her that I don't do my homework on a regular schedule like my brothers and sister. My grades are as good as theirs; what's her complaint?

A. Maybe her complaint is that your barging around the house in the small hours disturb *her* sleep. But as long as you creep around quietly, keep your grades up to snuff and manage to keep the circles from under your eyes, stay on your own schedule. It may be off-beat, but it seems to work for you.

Q. *We were just given our assigned reading list for our senior English class. When my mother saw it, she raised the roof. She says that some of the books aren't fit for a girl my age to read (I'm almost seventeen) and she says I'm not to read them, no matter what the teacher says. We have to read a minimum number or flunk the course. I feel surrounded. What should I do?*

A. If you can't make up the minimum number of books from those your mother approves, then suggest that your mother and your teacher settle the matter. Explain to your mother that you're in danger of flunking the course and ask that she arrange a conference with the teacher or write a letter, stating her position. Either the teacher can convince your mother that the books are suitable reading, after all, or she can suggest substitute books to fill out the requirements. Between them, the two adults should be able to work out a satisfactory compromise. And you don't even have to get in the line of fire!

Q. *I'm afraid I'm a doodler and a dawdler. Though I know I'm reasonably bright, I don't get very good grades. My classwork is O.K.; it's on homework that I run into trouble. I just can't settle down to do the two or three hours' bookwork that's necessary to get a decent grade in my school. I want to go to college, but I know I'll never make it at this rate.*

A. You say you have the mental equipment; maybe it's study equipment which you lack. Nobody can settle down to study properly unless there's a special work area, with all the paraphernalia near at hand. Make sure that you have a place to work—a desk or table in your room, the dining room table after the family dinner is over, the kitchen counter when the dishes are done for the night. Nearby should be everything you'll need: plenty of sharpened pencils, paper, a dictionary, reference books, a good reading light. Set yourself a time to begin work and make it the same time every evening. To help get started and keep going, promise yourself a reward: for instance, you'll take a break to watch a favorite TV show or listen to records if you've finished, to your satisfaction, a certain amount of work by a certain time. Studiously avoid all distractions: telephoning to get forgotten assignments (you won't need to if you carry an assignment pad inside your notebook), running to the refrigerator for an apple or a soft drink, cleaning out your briefcase (do *that* on weekends) or studying while listening to a disc jockey. Helpful desk accessories are a clock, and a calendar to keep track of dates special assignments are due. No matter how hard teachers try to cram facts into your head, the self-discipline necessary for good study habits is something only *you* can teach yourself.

Q. *I'm a sophomore in high school; my sister will be a freshman next year. All through school our parents have sent us to an expensive private academy. Everybody has to scrimp and save to make the tuition. We eat cheap food, my mother makes my sister's clothes and buys mine at a discount house, Dad is driving a five-year-old car and we can't afford any vacation except camping out. My sister and I would much rather switch to public school and have things a little easier financially. But my parents insist that a good education is the most important investment they can make for us. I'd like a little less education and a little more fun.*

A. Your parents undoubtedly surveyed the local school situation carefully before deciding to tighten their belts and live on a careful budget so they can afford private schooling. They'd probably like to kick up their heels, buy a new car, go out to dinner and the theater, plan a vacation in the Caribbean. But this seems less important to them than doing the best they can educationally for you two. Are you doing the best by yourself, and by them, by making the most of the expensive opportunity offered you? The time spent griping might better be spent studying. Make sure their investment pays off, in good grades and intellectual enrichment. The price your parents are paying is high. Don't cheat them—or yourself.

Q. *I get good marks but don't want to be considered a long-hair or a grind. When someone asks what I got on a test or my report card, I don't know what to say without sounding brainy or braggish.*

A. Try the truth, but not *all* the truth: "I didn't do too badly" or "I got a better mark than I expected; the test was so hard" or "I dream of getting a hundred, but I guess I'll never make it." And then turn the conversation away from yourself with "How about you? How did you do?" A narrow escape, but an escape!

Q. *In our family, as just about everywhere else these days, the pressure is on to get into college. Last year was miserable because my parents watched me like a pair of hawks to make sure I was studying hard and the days report cards came out were sheer torture. I work like a demon, but I just don't have the brains to make top grades. My parents won't believe it, though. They're both college graduates, and can't accept the fact that their son isn't as bright as they are. I can't stand another year of being on the spot.*

A. If you're really working up to your capacity (and your guidance counselor confirms it), then ask a faculty member to break the news to your parents that you're getting the top grades you're capable of. Once it's made clear to them that you can't do your best under constant pressure, perhaps they'll ease off a little. Just be sure they know (and you do, too) that you're doing your very best.

After-Class Queries

Q. *Last week, after gym period, a boy from our class burst into the girls' locker room and snapped a picture of several of us in various stages of semi-dress. He refuses to give us back the picture or the negative, and seems to think this is the greatest joke of the year. What can we do?*

A. If he won't give the picture and negative to you, perhaps he'll give them to the principal. Tell Shutter-bug you plan to report him, and see what develops.

Q. *I'm very interested in the study of foreign languages and want to join the French Club at school this year. The only trouble is that members are considered sort of long-hair and none is very popular. I've always been pretty well liked. I don't think I could stand the teasing from the guys if I joined up, even though I think I'd like the club.*

A. If the French Club stirs your interest, then by all means sign up, even though it doesn't have the status of some of the other extracurricular activities. You'll enjoy being with people who share your enthusiasm, though they may seem like off-beat types to your more lightweight friends. Maybe some of your friends will join, too, just to see what the club has to lure a popular guy like you.

Q. *In our school the washrooms are a disgrace. The school janitor does everything possible to keep them neat, but the kids don't seem to give a darn. We members of the student council would like some suggestions on how to alert the rest of the students to their responsibilities to keep paper towels off the floor and generally maintain neatness.*

A. Humor can help bring the results that nagging fails to achieve. Call a meeting of some of the funniest fellows and girls in your school and ask for suggestions for posters to be hung in the washrooms. Then turn the talented artists to work to produce the signs. Some schools, for instance, have kept paper towels off the floor by painting the outside of the waste cans to resemble basketball hoops and nets, and hanging a sign urging students to "Score a point for cleanliness!" Amazing how everyone's aim improved!

Q. *I've just entered a new high school in a small town for my senior year. I've overcome the disappointment I felt when my father was transferred by his firm and I found out I couldn't finish my last year with all my friends in the big city school I'd attended for the first three years. To complicate things, this is a very cliquey school; members of one group hardly even talk to others, and there's lots of rivalry. I don't know how to break into any one group, and I'm not sure I want to get involved with all the in-fighting. I don't want to be a lone wolf, either. I was popular and active in my old school. I just don't know what to do.*

A. Best advice is to take things slow and easy. Give yourself a couple of weeks to get the "feel" of the new school before you plunge into all sorts of activities. You'll have to be careful not to give the impression of a city slicker determined to take over the smaller school. Join one or two clubs, choosing those which genuinely interest you, rather than the ones which have the most popular members. Getting to know people individually through shared interests helps you to become friends more easily than trying to crash a crowd cold. You can't expect to be as big a wheel as you would have been in your old school (the old-time students, with three years seniority, have priority and are used to running things), but you can become an important part of your new school. You'll have a satisfying year, with enough new friends and activities to keep you busy and contented. As a late starter, who could ask for anything more?

Q. *For the past few weeks, many of the guys have been missing small items from their lockers: fountain pens, baseball mitts, lunch boxes. Nobody has been able to track down the thief. The other day I saw a guy I know, respected in school, open another boy's locker and take something out. Later that day the boy who uses the locker reported that his wallet was gone. I don't want to be a stool pigeon. What should I do?*

A. Report your information to your homeroom teacher or directly to the principal, asking that your name be kept quiet if possible. You owe it both to your classmates who are losing valuables and to the thief, who needs discipline or help, or both.

Q. *Our class is giving a variety show at school to help raise funds for new athletic equipment. I've been asked to perform, because the committee knows I've studied violin for years. The rest of the acts will be folk singers and comedy*

skits and tap dancing; I'd be the only long-hair attraction.
I'm afraid I'd be a real bomb, but I don't know how to get
out of doing the show. I've made it a point to be just one of
the guys, and never talk about my music, though I'm serious
about it and want to be a professional violinist.

A. Don't underestimate your classmates. They know you
play the violin, not the guitar, but they asked you anyway.
Ask your music teacher to suggest a piece of music with
popular appeal, and plunge ahead. Maybe you won't be the
hit of the show, but at least some of the group are going
to grow up to be your future audience. Play to them.

Q. *I'm fourteen and a high-school freshman. This summer*
one of the guys in our class took judo lessons and since
school opened he's been going around giving people "judo
chops," sharp blows with the side of the hand on the arm
or back or leg. I'm no sissy, but when he does this it hurts
so much that it makes tears come to my eyes. And the fad
is spreading. I don't want to be a fink, but I think it ought
to be stopped. I've heard that judo, wrongly used, can be
very dangerous. The teachers don't even seem to know
what's going on.

A. You're not being a fink by calling the matter to the
attention of school authorities. Judo, incorrectly and casually
used, can be very dangerous, as the boy must have been
told when he took lessons. Talk the problem over with the
school athletic coach or bring it up before the student
council. Perhaps a lecture before the school assembly by
a judo expert will alert everyone to the potential danger.
But don't maintain a stiff-upper-lip attitude of silence.
There's a possibility that you or a classmate could end up a
stiff, period.

Q. *I'm considered an athletic whiz and everyone is urging me to play on the school baseball team. I know I'm going to have to work like crazy to keep my grades up this semester, and I shouldn't take the time to play ball. But everyone says I owe it to the school, because we have a tough schedule this spring. I just don't know what to do.*

A. You owe your school loyalty and participation in extra-curricular activity only so far as those activities don't interfere with what you owe yourself: making the most of the opportunity to educate yourself. Your IQ is much more important than your batting average, both now and on your college or job application. So play it smart; don't "play ball"!

Q. *Up until this year I attended a private school with high entrance requirements. There was a no-nonsense attitude toward studying, and everyone was expected to be a good student. There was no onus involved in being a "grind." Family finances became rocky last summer and I had to transfer to a public school. There are many good students, of course, but they certainly aren't popular. Already I have a reputation for being a book hound, and the boys who are wheels on campus assume I'm not good date material, even though I'm quite pretty. Why do so many high-school students think brains exclude a pleasant personality or a sense of fun?*

A. Give up any idea of being prom queen, but don't change your study habits to pursue popularity. You'll find plenty of compatible spirits among the honor roll students in your new school. Though they may be labeled "greasy grinds" by some of the other pupils, you know from past experience that a bright personality often goes with a bright mind. Find your new friends among the scholars, continue to see the crowd from your old school and don't let your grades drop because you think such tactics might make your popularity soar.

Q. *Ever since school opened in the fall I've been writing the gossip column for the school paper—and I wish I'd never accepted the job. The paper comes out only once a month, and by the time it goes to press the romances I wrote about are usually on the rocks or it turns out I've linked couples who really can't stand each other. Everyone is miffed at me most of the time because they think I can't get the romantic facts straight. I can't resign. There's always been a School Scuttlebutt column in the paper and there'd be howls if it were given up. What can I do?*

A. Since your news on hot romances seems to be hopelessly inaccurate and out-of-date by the time the column appears, why not skip the whole gossip bit altogether? Make School Scuttlebutt a service column, running gripes from students about what they consider wrong with the school, along with suggestions for improvements. Make it a wailing wall and a sounding board. Such a column will be much more readable than warmed-over gossip, and of a great deal more value. A bit harder to write, maybe—but easier to live with.

Q. *I guess I'm just a born joiner and have been ever since grade school. I've had so much experience in club and school projects that I now have the reputation of being a leader, and it's got me in trouble. I realized the other day that I'm involved in a play at school, a choral recital at church and working on the school paper, on top of my homework and social life. My grades are going down like a lead balloon, and yet I don't know how to get out of any of these activities. People are counting on me.*

A. One of the people counting on you (and counting on his fingers the number of openings available in the freshman class) is the dean of admissions of the college of your choice. So you'd better jack those grades up, even though it means giving up one or more of the outside activities, or skipping dates until the play and choral recital are over. Not much fun, you say? Well, neither is being told "Sorry, no room!" when you apply for college.

Q. *After months of waiting and holding my breath, I've finally been invited to join a club of girls from our school. It's not exactly a sorority (those aren't allowed) but you have to be proposed by a member and voted on by the whole club. I was very excited until I discovered that, as part of the initiation, a new member is required to shoplift some small item from the dime store or drugstore to prove she has courage. These are all nice girls from good families, and I guess they all took something to become members. I don't approve, but I want to belong and I don't want to seem like a real square by refusing. What should I do?*

A. It will take even greater courage to stand up and announce firmly that you don't want any part of petty pilfering, for *any* reason. Maybe the girls will refuse to let you join their club. (Are you still so sure you want to hang around with these budding delinquents?) More likely they'll respect you for your gutsy honesty. In no case risk being brought into the police station as a law-breaker—that's not a very exclusive club. Even more dangerous is *not* being caught and thinking that you've managed to get away with something illegal and decidedly dishonest.

After Graduation, What?

Q. *My mother wants me to go to college, even though she knows that, ever since eighth grade, nursing school has been my objective. My mother say nurses work long, hard hours, don't get paid very much and have very little social status. She wants me to go to a fancy girls' school in the East. I will be graduated in six months, so I can't delay my decision much longer. Do I have to do what my mother tells me?*

A. Sing out your decision loud and clear: nursing school or nothing. If your mother puts the pressure on any says, "O.K., then nothing!" you may have to work your way through, although there are many scholarships available for student nurses. But it's more likely that your mother will respect you for your firmness and will withdraw her objections, once it's clear you'll make no career compromise. Be prepared to fight for what you want; don't be surprised if you don't have to.

Q. *I've been in love with a boy for over a year, since we both started our senior year in high school. Now he's going away to college and I'm staying at home to work, since my family can't afford to send me to college. I think I'll marry the boy after he graduates from the university, but I worry about his getting too smart for me. I don't want him to out-grow me, with his education and wider experience, even before we're married.*

A. Though you can't go to college yourself, you can work at enlarging your store of knowledge. You'll have plenty of time for reading on those dateless nights during the college year. Set yourself a program of self-education through books. Your high-school English teacher or an interested librarian can give you a suggested reading list. Enroll in a Great Books course in your town. Check on adult education courses and college night school opportunities. Read a daily newspaper and a weekly news magazine conscientiously. If you keep aware that every new experience and every new bit of information helps you to grow intellectually, you won't risk being outgrown by your guy, college education or not.

Q. *My dad is a real do-it-yourself addict, even when it comes to education. The other day he announced he'll pay my way through two years of college, but after that I'm on my own to win a scholarship or earn my way. He says if I really want an education, it's up to me to prove it by working for it. Just because he's a self-made man, who slaved his way through college, he expects me to do the same. His only concession is that he'll lend me the money for my last two years, at 3½ per cent interest! What gets me is that he could afford to send me to the most expensive school in the country if he wanted to. What do you make of a guy like that?*

A. Exactly what he made of himself, a hard-headed, hard-working guy who doesn't want his son to become soft by having life handed to him on a solid silver platter. He's teaching you a lesson that you won't necessarily learn in school: that the things you value most are those you've earned yourself. Check the statistics on the average annual income of college graduates vs. non-graduates, and then take him up on that loan offer. You'll be able to pay that 3½ per cent interest many times over out of your increased earnings.

Q. *My dad is determined to have me attend his alma mater, and he keeps nagging me to keep my grades up so I'll be eligible. I don't want to go to his school. I want to be an engineer, and his university doesn't have the best engineering department. I can't get him to understand. It makes me so mad I just want to quit trying. If I'm not eligible because of bad grades, at least that will end the argument!*

A. If you can't convince your dad, then bring up the big guns, someone whose judgment he can't ignore. Try your school guidance counselor or an alumnus of the university of your choice, one who is familiar with the excellence of the engineering department there. Someone must convince your father that attending a school which doesn't offer the courses you want is a disastrous waste of your time and his money. If he can't be swayed, then check into the possibilities of scholarships and ways of working your way through school. Once your dad sees how serious you are about your choice of a college, he'll almost inevitably change his mind—and respect yours.

Q. *I'm going away for my freshman year at college this month, up to my ears in advice and instructions from my parents, who are scared to see their darling daughter out of the nest for the first time. I know they're concerned about my welfare, but I think they're over-protective. For instance, I have strict orders to phone home, collect, every Thursday night at eight o'clock to let them know how things are going. I hate to be tied down like a silly little girl. I thought part of going to college was to learn to take care of yourself.*

A. Those telephone wires aren't necessarily apron strings.

You needn't declare total independence the minute you board the train for college. Give your parents a chance to realize, slowly, that you can take care of yourself. For the first few Thursdays, put in that call (you may be feeling homesick and delighted at the chance for family contact). Later on, reassure your folks by letter, scheduled to arrive on Thursday morning, that all goes well but that you won't be calling that night. Part of going to college is learning to take care of yourself, it's true. But another part is learning to take care of the feelings of other people.

Q. *I can't afford to go to college. My teachers say I'm excellent college material and would get into any school where I applied, but they don't seem to be able to count: I have four younger brothers and sisters, my dad earns a small salary, and there's barely enough to scrape by on now. I'd do anything for more education (I want to be a chemist) but it isn't possible.*

A. You can't afford *not* to go to college! Aside from the personal satisfaction and intellectual growth provided by higher education, college training increases your earning power enormously. College graduates earn an estimated $100,000 to $250,000 more in their working lifetime than their high-school graduate counterparts. How are you going to swing it if the family can't help? Scholarships are one answer. Write to all of the colleges you're interested in for detailed information on scholarship opportunities there. Inquire about possible apprentice scholarships stemming from the large chemical companies. Check your school guidance counselor for local scholarship offerings; often fraternal groups, women's clubs, civic organizations, PTA's, etc., have grants available. Write your state department of education in the capital; most states offer some sort of scholarship money to worthy and needful students. Investigate the grants of the National Merit Scholarship Corporation (1580 Sherman Avenue, Evanston, Illinois) and the General Motors National Scholarship Plan (c/o Educational Testing Service, Princeton, New Jersey). Often companies offer aid to the children of their employees. Have your father ask the personnel department of his firm if you qualify for assistance.

You can help pay your way through college by working, of course. College students as a group earn one-fourth of their educational expenses. You can average $300 annually, working ten to twelve hours weekly during the school year. College men earn an average of $500 during summer vacation, girls, $275.

Don't overlook the possibilities of borrowing to finance your education. Most colleges have loan funds, with low interest rates. Uusually only the payment of interest is required during the student's time at college, with the principal being repaid in reasonable installments over a long period (ranging from six to ten years, for instance) after graduation.

For detailed information on all the financial aid available to students who have everything necessary for college entrance except money, check the files of your local library for the excellent article, "You *Can* Afford College," in the January 6, 1962, issue of the *Saturday Evening Post*. You owe yourself a college education. Don't let yourself down.

Q. *How can I get a message through my father's thick skull? He wants me to attend the same Ivy League school he did. I'm a junior in high school now and, though I study hard, my counselor says that, with my grades, I have very little chance of getting into Dad's university. The truth is, the lower half of the class in his time wouldn't be admitted anymore. But just try to explain this to him. He's after me all the time.*

A. Your guidance counselor can make clear to your father the new academic facts of life: higher entrance requirements, more students applying, just not enough room for all the sons of "old boys." Once your father meets the facts head-on, he'll probably stop strangling you with the old school tie and take a more realistic view of your capabilities and college chances. But if he refuses to accept your counselor's judgment, go ahead and apply for entrance anyhow. When the dean of admissions says, "Sorry, wrong college!" there's no more to be said.

Q. *I'm a high-school junior and dying to see more of the world, both to learn what I'll never get out of geography and history books and to help promote world understanding. I really want to get to know different countries, their people, their history, their culture, firsthand. My family has promised me a summer abroad as a graduation present. I want to make the most of it. Do you have any suggestions?*

A. Hosteling may be the answer for you, since it provides an inexpensive, leisurely way to travel with a congeinal group through a country and get to know the people. Hosteling trips are available in European, Asian and South American countries, as well as in all fifty states. For information, write American Youth Hostels, Inc., 14 West 8th Street, New York 11, New York.

The Experiment in International Living, a non-profit group, founded in 1932, is designed to promote world understanding through "home-stays" in foreign countries. American students live for a month with families abroad, then spend two or three weeks traveling, usually with a member of the host family, in the chosen country. Under the plan, foreign students enjoy the same hospitality in America. The Experiment accepts students with outstanding leadership qualities, a reputation for getting along with people, and special achievements in personal interests. A knowledge of the language of the country to be visited is sometimes required; some scholarships and loans are available. For full details, write The Experiment in International Living, Putney, Vermont.

Other sources of information for foreign travel for young people: Vacations Abroad, $1.25, from UNESCO Publications, 801 Third Avenue, New York 22, New York, and Work-Study-Travel Abroad, $1, from N.S.A., 20 West 38th Street, New York 18, New York.

Q. *The bottom has just dropped out of my world. I've always wanted to go to a certain very good girls' school in the East and have worked and slaved all through high school to keep my marks high and to be a "well-rounded student." I knew it was tough to get into your first-choice college, but I was counting on making the grade. I've been turned down by the school, and by my second- and third-choice colleges as well. My marks were good, but not good enough, I guess. I don't know where to turn.*

A. An increasing number of students with your problem are turning to the College Admissions Center in Evanston, Illinois, a non-profit organization founded in 1958 to help scholar meet school. It's harder and harder each year to get into big "name" schools, because the number of qualified applicants has soared. Even students with good academic and extracurricular records may be turned down because a school is seeking to diversify the geographic backgrounds of its students. Even though the "Sorry—Full" signs are up at many top schools, there are excellent smaller colleges with vacancies, but too often the college-bound high-schooler doesn't know about them. The C.A.C. acts as middleman to bring the two together. The fee to students is only $10. Submit your application, with high-school transcripts, personal ratings and a photograph. These are made available to more than two hundred participating colleges and universities. Though the Center doesn't guarantee college admission or recommend students to colleges, more than half the applicants have been matched with a college right for them. In 1961, the average C.A.C. registrant received letters of interest from twelve schools. College Admissions Center may be able to provide the happy ending to your sad story.

8 : *Jobs*

Getting a Job

Q. *Last year, when I went looking for a summer job in May, every position was filled. I don't want to be stuck again this year. Is March or April too early to start hunting? And where should a teen-ager look?*

A. Since there are many more teens looking for summer jobs than there are part-time positions to be filled, early springtime certainly isn't too early to line up vacation work. Start by asking your parents and their friends if they know of openings. Check the neighborhood businesses—drugstore, supermarket, filling station, etc.—for positions. Query your guidance counselor or school placement officer on possibilities for work as clerk, messenger, office boy. And don't overlook the Help Wanted section of the newspaper, a source of information on job availabilities that a surprising number of teen-agers ignore. Before applying for a job, check to find out what papers are necessary (work permit, social security card, letters of reference, etc.) and bring them with you.

Even if you don't land a regular job, you can be your own

boss this summer. Go to work for neighbors as car washer, grass cutter, dog walker, or baby-sitter. Hire out as house-watcher and plant-waterer for people going on vacation. There's plenty of work to be done by ambitious, hard-working teen-agers who know where to look for jobs or who offer desired services on an hourly basis.

Q. *I'm fifteen years old and would like to have a baby-sitting job. Do you think I'm old enough to be hired? And how would I go about finding a job? Do you have any suggestions for being a good sitter? I have two younger brothers, so I'm used to children and good with them.*

A. To get the job: canvass your neighborhood, ringing the doorbells of families with young children to offer your services. You might invest in some printed business cards (they're inexpensive) giving your name, address, telephone number and rates. Add, in the lower corner, "References" and be prepared to have anxious mothers phone your school principal, your minister and/or people you've worked for to check up on you. To keep the job: arrive on time, ask the mother exactly what's expected of you (using a notebook to write down your instructions if they're long or complicated). Be sure to have the phone number of the children's doctor, the fire department, a helpful neighbor and the place where the parents can be reached in an emergency. Ask if you have refrigerator privileges, and how extensive they are. (You're usually welcome to peanut butter sandwiches and a soft drink, but *not* to left-over cold roast beef or the little unopened jar of caviar tucked in the back corner!) You shouldn't be expected to do household chores (not at 50¢ an hour!), but you are responsible for doing the dishes if you feed the children, hanging up their clothes and neatening the bathroom if you bathe them, and cleaning up any mess you make. No visitors, unless you have permission to have a girl friend drop by to keep you company; no lengthy phone calls. For your own sake, don't accept sitting assignments stretching past eleven o'clock, except on Fridays and Saturdays, when you can sleep late in the morning. And make delivery to your front door when the job is over part of the deal. You're in business!

Q. *I'm a boy, seventeen, with summer camp counselor experience. Recently, a woman in our neighborhood, with three small sons, asked me to come to work for her on Saturdays. I wouldn't be a baby-sitter, exactly; she wants someone to teach her boys to swim and play baseball and stuff like that. Her husband is overseas with the army and the boys don't get much male companionship or instruction. I'd enjoy the job (they're nice kids), but I worry about what my buddies would say about my playing "nursemaid."*

A. Your friends made no comments when you went off to your camp counselor job; they're not likely to do so now. But you can refer to your new job as a sort of "day camp" when you talk about it, just to stave off any smart cracks.

Q. *Ever since I was in fourth grade my parents have given me piano lessons, in hopes that I'd be a concert pianist. I've practiced faithfully and really worked hard because it seemed to mean so much to them. But my heart has never really been in it. I do, however, like jazz and play a pretty mean jazz piano. I've been offered the chance to play with a jazz combo this summer at a resort hotel, and I'm dying to accept. The job pays well and it's the sort of music that really gets to me. My parents are all shook up at the idea.*

They think I'd be wasting my talent and all the years of hard work. How can I convince them?

A. Eventually, your parents are going to have to realize that they can't choose your career for you. The disappointment may be hard for them to take, but they'll have to face it sooner or later. Why not sooner, this summer? Explain to them how much satisfaction you get from jazz, throw in a few well-chosen words about jazz being the "native American folk music" and then accept the job offer. It's your life and to live it happily, you have to choose the career which satisfies *you.*

Q. *A movie company is making a film on location in our small town and I've been bitten badly by the acting bug. I've been asked to be an extra in some crowd scenes and I have the feeling I can make an impression. I want to ask the director if he thinks I have a chance for success in movies. What's your advice?*

A. Go ahead and ask the director—if you can get close enough to talk to him. Then, whatever his answer, decide to finish high school and preferably college, too, before assaulting Hollywood's golden gates. Put in plenty of time at little theater projects and school dramatics, but don't neglect the book learning. The more knowledgeable you are, the better you'll be able to play any role. We're assuming you want to be an *actress,* not just a *star.* There's a big difference!

Q. *I'd like to go into the advertising business, and wonder what chance there is for a fellow to get a spot in an agency for the summer. I'm sixteen, in the second half of my junior year in high school, and have college plans. I make good grades and am very active in school activities. What are my chances?*

A. Advertising is one of "glamour" careers, and summer jobs in agencies are at a premium. Best idea is to spend this summer doing some sort of selling work—in a department store, a supermarket, a pharmacy, even door-to-door—to find out firsthand what people buy, and why. (One top ad agency insists that its executives spend time periodically in direct contact with customers, clerking in stores or filling stations, so that they don't lose touch with the people they're selling to through advertising campaigns.)

Put the agency job on your "position wanted" schedule for *next* summer. You'll have three months of selling (and that's what advertising really is) to list under "experience" on your application blank. Early next spring, write to the head of personnel of the ad agencies in your city. A phone call will find out the name of the department head, and a personally addressed letter makes a more favorable impression. Outline your school background and describe the work you did the previous summer. Mention that you plan to make advertising a career after college, list business and personal references, and ask for an appointment for an interview. The letter will be your first important practical test in the field of advertising. See if you can sell *yourself!*

Q. *I'm fifteen and (I think) a budding actress. I've performed in school plays and little theater groups and everyone has said I'm really good. Now I have an offer to do a local TV dramatic show. My parents want me to finish high school, at least, before I decide on making acting my career. But I've thought and dreamed for so long about being an actress that I can't bear to turn down this chance.*

A. Your mind sounds pretty firmly made up, and this may be the chance to take the first giant step toward realizing your ambition. You must have thought about the sacrifices you'll have to make for an acting career, especially one begun so young. You'll miss much of the fun of high-school life, but if you care enough about your dream, this won't be too important to you. Your parents are right, of course, about finishing high school. You'll have to attend classes or be tutored until you're sixteen, but don't consider that you'll be simply fulfilling a legal requirement or marking time. Everything you learn, everything you experience, in school and out, contributes to your craft. The more you know, the better actress you'll be—and you and your parents and your audience will be the happier for it.

Q. *I want to work this summer and I've begun to look for a job. The catch is, I plan to go on vacation with my family in August, provided my dad's time off comes through on schedule. It may be that the family will stay home this summer and my folks go off together in the fall. When I apply for a job, I don't know whether to tell the boss that I might quietly disappear near the end of the summer. Is honesty really the best policy?*

A. Since you're not certain whether you'll be on the job all summer long, whether you tell the boss the whole story depends on the kind of job you're trying to land. If it's a routine chore (delivery boy, stock boy at a supermarket, etc.), then accept the job, planning to give adequate notice when and if you do go on vacation. However, if it's work which requires training and an investment of the firm's money and time before you're of value to them, then it's only honest to mention, before accepting the job, that there's a chance you won't be able to remain for the whole summer. To do anything less would be as dishonest as short-changing the customers or dipping into the cash register.

On-the-Job Straining

Q. *If I expect to go to college in the fall, I have to work this summer and save like mad. The thing that tilts me is that most of my friends come from well-to-do families and don't have to take jobs. They'll spend their summer playing tennis, lounging around the beach and having a rare old time while I'm working. I can't help being resentful.*

A. After college, you may look back and count yourself luckier than your friends. Adversity can be man's best friend, and unearned prosperity a handicap. A lot of kids who play now pay later by not having learned how to work early enough in life. They're the kind who often end up working for *your* kind.

Q. *I'm sixteen and baby-sit to earn extra cash. I don't like to sit past eleven o'clock on a school night, because it's too hard to get up early, so I've told everyone I sit for that I want to be home early. One couple always promises to get home on time, but they never make it. The other night I dozed off on the couch and was asleep when they got home at twelve-thirty. They were mad because I wasn't wide-awake and alert. They almost refused to pay me! Do they have a right to gripe?*

A. It's never wise for a baby-sitter to fall asleep on the job. She usually doesn't have the built-in alarm system that mothers possess, which wakes her up at the sound of a cough or a blanket being kicked off. But since you'd made it clear that you wanted to be home at a certain hour, the parents have no real complaint. Cross them off your sitting list, and tell them why.

Q. *This summer I have a job as a waitress in a drive-in restaurant. Our uniform is a scoop-neck peasant blouse, shorts and a frilly apron. The outfit is no more revealing than sport clothes most girls wear (I don't feel self-conscious in it and even my very strict father doesn't disapprove). But the male customers act as if the waitresses were a bunch of easy marks. Boy's I've known in school act entirely different when then come in as customers and seem constantly on the make. I'm still the same "nice girl" I always was. How do I make the customers (especially the fellows I know) realize this? Don't suggest I quit my job; we get a bonus at the end of the summer if we stay all season, and I need the money.*

A. Males on the make get tired of the game if the quarry doesn't react. Your best defense is simply to ignore offensive cracks. Don't get huffy, don't act insulted, don't give them the what-makes-you-think-I'm-that-kind-of-girl? routine. Just hold your tongue and your temper, take their order and think about that end-of-the-summer bonus. Every job has its occupational hazards!

Q. *Last month I baby-sat for a young couple who had given me permission to invite a girl friend to keep me company. The other day the mother asked me about charges for a long-distance call made on that evening. I knew I hadn't called anyone but I finally pried out of my friend the admission that she'd sneaked a call to her boy friend in the Navy while I was giving the baby its ten o'clock feeding. I*

can't afford to pay for the call (it came to more than $7). My girl friend says she doesn't have the cash, but I feel responsible. What will I do?

A. First, strike the girl from your list of favorite (and honest) people. Then explain what happened to the woman, and apologize. Tell her you want to pay for the call but don't have the cash on hand. Then offer to sit, at the usual hourly rates, until you've worked off the debt. You won't make an honest woman out of your friend, but you *will* regain the respect and trust of your employer.

Q. *I work after school at the drugstore where the kids from school hang out. My problem is that my girl hangs around too much during business hours. She pretends she's just there to have a soda or buy a magazine or meet a friend, but the boss is beginning to get wise. I try to ignore her or treat her just like any other customer, but she gets hurt feelings if I don't pay attention to her. I'm stumped.*

A. Tell your girl that you have a funny feeling in your wallet that you might be fired if she continues to hang around. She can't feel hurt if she's getting the brush from your boss, not from you. You can soften the blow by making a date to have a Coke with her the minute you get off duty. Step round to the other side of the fountain and become a paying customer!

Q. *I've been baby-sitting regularly for a young couple in our neighborhood every Saturday night. They trust me and depend on me. Next Saturday night I've been invited to a formal dance at the country club by a very special boy, and I want desperately to go. The sticker is that the young couple is also planning to go. If I break my sitting date, I'm afraid they'll have trouble getting someone else. What should I do?*

A. Call the young mother and explain why you can't show up on Saturday night. Have at hand the names of two or three of your competent gal pals who can take over the sitting chores, in case she asks for your suggestions about a substitute. But don't feel too badly about leaving her in the lurch. Usually, young parents have a willing grandmother or aunt in the background for just such emergencies!

Q. *I work after school as a delivery boy for a neighborhood drugstore. I don't get much in the way of salary; most of the money comes from tips. Lots of girls I go to school with live around here and sometimes they answer the door when I'm delivering packages. I feel real funny accepting money from them. How can a guy ask a girl out for a date after he's had his hand out for a tip?*

A. How can a fellow *afford* to ask a girl out if he doesn't assume a "business as usual" attitude when he's working? The girls realize that you're earning part of your income from tips; they'll get their money back when you ask them for dates.

Q. *My best girl friend baby-sits for spending money two or three nights a week. She doesn't like to be alone at night, so she invites me along to keep her company. At first I didn't mind, but I just realized I'm playing the sucker. We'll be watching TV when the baby wakes for its bottle and she says, "I don't want to miss this part—feed the kid, will you?" I end up doing most of the work and she gets all the money. How unfair can you be?*

A. Don't just sit there—baby-sit on your own! As long as you're putting in the hours, might as well pick up the cash. Be "too busy" to keep your gal pal company; let her do the work she's paid for.

Q. *When I baby-sit, I usually get ravenous about ten o'clock, out of boredom, I guess. The other night I was sitting for a young couple and made myself a sandwich of cold meat and cheese, and had a glass of milk and a piece of cake to top it off. The parents came home unexpectedly in the middle of my snack, and though the woman didn't say anything, I got the impression that she was annoyed. Was what I did so awful?*

A. Unless you've been given specific permission, the refrigerator is off limits on baby-sitting jobs. You wouldn't think of trying on the woman's clothes or using her makeup; neither should you feel free to help yourself to food un- invited. If boredom hits you in the stomach mid-evening, plan ahead and pack a lunch. Most young marrieds operate on a tight budget and you ate a big hole right through it!

Q. *Last summer I worked in an office for a friend of my father, and, though I made a good salary, I wasn't very happy there. The man is over fifty and set in his ways. Whenever I suggested a new way of doing things, he just smiled tolerantly and said, "When you're a little older, you'll understand the old ways are the best ways." My dad thinks I should take the same job again this year. I don't think I can stand it, even though I can't earn as much anywhere else and its the work I want to do when I get out of college.*

A. You sound like a young man in a hurry, eager to get out and change the world. But world-beaters have to realize that they must work within the framework that exists; dramatic changes are usually not possible overnight. In fact, they're often not desirable. You may have fresh new ideas that might be useful in the business; you may also have ideas that seem new to you, but which are old stuff, tried and found wanting, to the boss. Try the job again. Make your suggestions in a more tentative fashion ("This seems like a good idea to me. What do you think?"). Then listen—and learn. You have a marvelous chance to learn a business from the ground up, to find out which techniques have worked and which have failed, to profit from the experiences of older people. Most important, for this job and future ones, you'll learn to work with people. That's a talent you'll need in your personal and business life forever.

Q. *I began baby-sitting two years ago, when I was thirteen. Because I was young and only took care of kids after they were put to bed for the night, I charged 35¢ an hour, though the older girls asked 50¢ or even 75¢. I have a lot of steady customers, but now that I'm older, I do lots more work, often feeding the young ones and putting them to bed. Sometimes the mother even leaves the dinner dishes for me to do, and some of the ironing. And I'm still getting 35¢ an hour! I don't know how to raise my rates without losing customers.*

A. Hey! Slavery was abolished a century ago! It's time you were paid the going rates for your locality. If face-to-face financial dealings make you shy and tongue-tied, then send out letters to your regular customers advising them that you're upping your hourly charge. Give them the reasons for this. As long as you continue to be a dependable, hard-working sitter, you won't get any complaints. No one knows better than young parents that the cost of living, even for sitters, has gone up.

Q. *When I was baby-sitting the other night, the doorbell rang and a high-school boy from the apartment across the hall sauntered in when I opened the door. He acted as if he owned the place, made himself at home, settled down to watch TV with me, and even helped himself to a soft drink from the refrigerator. The parents came home early and after the boy left they spoke sharply to me about entertaining guests when they were out. I thought he was their friend. I didn't know how to keep him out.*

A. If you can't manage to keep strangers out of the house when you're baby-sitting, you're not up to the job. The parents were right to be annoyed. It's a wise policy not to let *anyone* past the front door unless the parents have told you ahead of time that they're expecting someone. It's a simple matter to say, with your hand firmly on the door-knob and a foot braced to keep the door from being opened, "I'm sorry, the Simpsons aren't at home, but if you'll give me your name, I'll be glad to tell them you were here." Get the name and then close the door, quickly and firmly, locking it. You're the baby-sitter, not a substitute hostess.

Q. *I'm one of two girls, both sixteen, who work after classes at a soda fountain near school. We get paid pretty good wages, and I take my job seriously. I'd think it was almost like stealing not to work hard. The other girl goofs off all the time. She makes a great show of working hard when the manager is around, but the rest of the time she flirts with the boy customers, sits in the back booth and reads movie magazines, or just leans against the counter, watching*

*me wash glasses. It makes me mad, because I end up doing
a lot of her work. What can I do?*

A. You can keep on working hard and wait for the girl's
laziness and the boss to catch up with her. On-the-job loafing
won't go unnoticed forever. When it's time to cut costs, first
to go will be the gal who cut corners.

Q. *Well, it happened again! I went to baby-sit for the first
time for a young couple with two small children, and found
the dinner dishes stacked in the sink. As the mother waltzed
out the door, she said, "You won't mind doing the dishes
and folding the laundry while we're gone, will you?" I
always seem to get caught like this. For 50¢ an hour, should
I really do housework? I never know what to say when I'm
asked to do extra chores—and I end up doing them.*

A. Next time you get an over-the-shoulder request to do
a little light housekeeping along with the moppet-tending,
say, "Of course, I'd be glad to. I charge $1 an hour when I
do housework, too. Is that all right?" The requests to do
dishes and iron and neaten up the living room will disappear
like magic.

Q. *I'm working on Saturdays at a sports shop in our
neighborhood. Lots of the guys stop in to browse, chat with
me, and so on. But they end up horsing around, making a
lot of noise and disturbing the paying customers. These guys
never buy anything, and I'm afraid my boss is getting mad.
But I don't know how to make them leave.*

A. Don't try to cope with the problem when you're on
the job. Instead, explain things to the fellows, one or two at
a time, during the week, letting them know their antics are

endangering your job. If that doesn't work, tell your boss you can't discourage the guys from coming in and ask him to deal with the situation. Better he throws *them* out than throws *you* out.

Q. *We live in a new, sparsely settled subdevelopment, and I'm a little bit afraid to baby-sit. I'm the sort of person who thinks every little creak or rattle is a burglar. But I need the money. My boy friend has offered to come along on sitting jobs to keep me company, but my mother says this wouldn't look right. What should I do?*

A. Earn your extra folding money in some nice, brightly lit drugstore or supermarket and leave the baby-sitting in dark and lonely areas to hardier souls. Your mother's right; it wouldn't be proper to take your guy along to hold your hand. You're supposed to be baby-sitting, but who's the baby?

Q. *Is it all right to have girl friends drop in to visit me while I'm baby-sitting? I sit two or three nights a week, often on weekends, and therefore I don't get as much chance as I'd like to see my friends.*

A. The answer is "Yes, if . . ." And the list of if's is long: *If* you get the parents' permission ahead of time, *if* you don't have more than two guests at the most, *if* you are all neat and tidy (no furniture out of place, magazines flung about, icebox raids), *if* your giggling and chatter doesn't interfere in any way with moppet-minding.

Q. *This summer I'm working as a typist and filing clerk in a small business office. I'm seventeen, just out of high school, and most of the other employees are middle-aged. They all call each other by their first names, the boss included. Even the office boy, who is only about a year older than I am, is on this casual basis with everyone. I don't know what's expected of me. I'd feel funny referring to my boss as Jerry instead of Mr. Perkins, but it seems stuffy to be the only one acting formal and calling everybody Mr.*

A. You're a special case: you're a new employee, you're younger than the rest of the group and you're a girl. Play it smart and respectful, calling everyone (with the exception of the teen-aged office boy) Mr. or Sir. Some offices pride themselves on their easy informality, and the boss may ask you to unbend and get on a first-name basis. But a lady waits until she's asked!

Q. *I baby-sit, not just for fun, but practically for a living, since my family can't afford to give me much allowance. One couple I work for never has the right change and each night they end up owing me till next time. Likely as not, by "next time" they've forgotten all about it and I'm too shy to remind them. What can I do? I need the money.*

A. Baby-sitting is a business, and your attitude has to be businesslike and efficient. Do one of two things. Either carry enough jingling money so you can give change from a $5 bill or, when they plead temporary poverty, call their bluff by saying, "That's all right; I'll stop over to pick up the money on my way home from school tomorrow." You earned your pay; make sure you get it.

Career Challenges

Q. *I'm a junior in high school, hope to go to college but haven't the foggiest notion what I want to do with my life. My dad's a doctor, but that life doesn't appeal to me. Most of the other guys I know are dead certain what career they*

*want to follow, but I just can't decide. I figure it's about time
I made up my mind.*

A. Aptitude tests may provide a signpost by indicating the
kind of work you'd be good at. But you'll still have to follow
your heart. (A top advertising man I know took an aptitude
test when he came out of college and was told he should
go into factory management or be a jazz musician. The test
results hinted that advertising was one of the last careers he
should attempt. But it was what he *wanted* to do, and he
took the plunge in spite of what the tests showed. He has
never been sorry and neither have his clients!) Try to think
what kind of work you'd be eager to get to in the morning
and reluctant to leave at night. Doctor, lawyer, merchant,
chief—you have to *like* what you're doing to excel at it.
Read about various careers, talk to businessmen friends of
your family, get to know as much as possible about as many
different professions as possible. One day the lightning will
strike; you'll say to yourself, *"That's* for me!"—and you're
on your way. *Who's Who in American Business,* look out!

Q. *I'm nineteen, one of five guys in a summer trainee
program in a local firm. We work there during school vacations, learning the business from the ground up. The idea is
that, after college graduation, we'll be ready to go to work
full-time in a junior executive spot. I want to get the best
job that opens up. I do everything I'm told and do it well,
but after two summers there's no indication from the boss
that I'm any better than the other fellows. How can I make
myself number one prospect?*

A. "Doing what you're told" is, of course, essential on any
job. But doing the extra things you haven't been told to do,
but which you know need doing, can make you number one

man on the totem pole. Every day on the job do something which *isn't* required. Work an extra hour, ask an extra question, make an extra suggestion, read or write an extra memo. Don't be pushy; play it quiet. Let your work speak for you— but let it speak in an affirmative, authoritative fashion. Hard work and long hours and an additional measure of initiative —that's what successful junior executives are made of!

Q. *Don't laugh at me, but I want to be a musical comedy writer. I'm seventeen, a high-school senior and have already written the words, music and book for two musicals put on by our high-school drama society. Both were so successful that extra performances had to be scheduled to meet the ticket demand. I'm wondering if I can make it in the big time. I know it's an awful risk, but I sure want to try.*

A. *Do* you have a chance on Broadway? You'll never know unless you try. First, if at all possible, put in four years at a good college, one with an excellent music and drama department. Then, try your luck in the big time. Even if you don't make it, you'll be happier half-starving in a cold water walk-up and *trying* than in a nice, safe, comfortable job, wondering for the rest of your life if you could have hit it big.

Q. *More than anything else in the world, I want to be a writer. I'm a fifteen-year-old girl and my English teacher says she thinks I show great promise. But she's the only one in our small town who understands this yearning, burning desire of mine. What can I do all by myself to fulfill my dream?*

A. If you want to be a writer, then read a lot—and write a lot. Devour the good writers, from Shakespeare to Salinger. Immerse yourself in written words; let them seep in through your eyes and emotions and pores. And write! Don't just *think* about writing or *talk* about writing or *dream* about writing. *Write.* Keep a daily journal. Get down in words what you've seen and done and felt and thought each day. Write something every day, whether you feel like it or not. Writing is a solitary occupation and requires enormous self-discipline.

Don't write for yourself alone. Work for the school paper and literary magazine. Enter every essay contest and creative writing competition that comes along. Send your best work to magazines, big and small. (One practical hint: make sure those manuscripts are neatly typed, double-spaced, with fresh ribbon on pristine paper. A busy editor might not give your work all the attention it may merit because it isn't neat enough to look "important.") If you write the Great American Novel, don't let it languish unseen in your desk drawer. Send it to publishers. In recent years the work of several teen-aged novelists has been published, some with excellent critical notices. Even if you get stacks of rejection slips, you may also get an occasional editorial comment or criticism that will help you, or a word of praise and encouragement that keeps you going. Sound hard? It is. But big dreams are not cheaply bought.

Q. *I'm eighteen, a college sophomore, an honor student during high-school days and on the dean's list in college. Already, recruiting teams from corporations have been interviewing me for employment after graduation. I've never heard so much talk about retirement plans, fringe benefits, stock participation, etc., in my life. I have the feeling I'm going to be enveloped in a big, safe corporate nest as soon as I graduate. But the prospects of a steadily growing income look good. On the other hand, a friend and I have an idea for starting a business after college. My father thinks I should take the secure offers from one of the big companies. I'm inclined to gamble on a business of my own. What do you think?*

A. Check your history book. It's full of stories of brave men who had the courage to rely on their own brains and talent. The risk in going into business for yourself should be a stimulant, not a deterrent. Risk is good for the circulation, especially above the neck. And even if you should come a cropper, there are always the more safe, secure corporation jobs to fall back on. But while you're young, without having to worry about mortgage payments and dentist bills and groceries for a family of five, why not go for broke?

Q. *I'm going to work soon for a good company in the career field I've chosen for myself. I'm determined to be a business success. Is there any sure-fire formula?*

A. A wise and successful man once said that business success rests on a tripod: the *ability* to do the job, the *desire* to do the job and the ability to *get along with people* while doing it. If any one of the legs of the tripod is missing, chances of reaching top rank diminish. Ability to do the job includes native talents and a capacity to keep on learning and growing, staying abreast of new developments in your field, constantly adding to your knowledge from on-the-job activity and corollary reading. The desire is important because no human being does well what he doesn't *enjoy* doing. Enthusiasm for your job must remain fresh and vital; when you're bored with your work, your work immediately shows it. And since you'll always be working with people, it's essential to be able to work together congenially, to accept orders from superiors, to delegate authority to those working under you, to extract the best effort from co-workers. (One of the greatest accolades accorded the late, great fashion editor Carmel Snow: "She made you achieve more than you could.") None of this is easy. But success isn't easy to come by.

Q. *I live in a little town in the sticks and long to get away and see the world. I've daydreamed about becoming an airline stewardess when I get out of high school, but I don't have any idea what the qualifications are. Can you fill me in?*

A. Basic requirements vary slightly with different airlines, but these are typical: you must be twenty to twenty-seven years old, unmarried (though childless widows and divorcees may qualify), 5′ 2″ to 5′ 9″ and weigh between 100 and 140 pounds, proportionate to your height. Your vision must be at least 20/50 without glasses, your physical appearance pleasant and your grooming good. High-school graduation is a requisite, and many lines prefer additional college work and/or business experience. You'll be trained for your new work at the airline's expense in an intensive four- to six-week course at a stewardess training center; some lines provide a trainee salary, others do not. At the completion of your course, you receive your wings and go to work. The job has many pluses: opportunity to travel and meet new people, moderate working hours, plenty of time to browse around on your own and relax, a yearly travel allowance, discounts on other airlines, vacations with pay. You'll be assigned to a home base city wherever you're needed, but the airlines try to take your preference into consideration. And there's always the opportunity to advance. Write to the airline of your choice for more detailed information on its program of stewardess training. The sky's the limit for your future.

Q. *I live in a small city in the mid-West and have dreams of becoming a model. I'm considered very pretty and many of my friends say I'm better-looking than girls in magazines. I'm sixteen. Is there any hope for me?*

A. To become a successful model requires 4 F's: Face, Figure, Flair—and Fate. "Just another pretty face" is not enough. You need good bone structure which photographs well (do you look better in the flesh than in the flash bulb pictures?). You need a lean figure, since the camera adds poundage; you must be above average in height (between

5′ 5″ and 5′ 9½″). Flair includes a fashion sense, a certain dramatic ability (could you look warm and gay and fun on the beach in a bathing suit in mid-March?), a liveliness that comes through in photos. And Fate means that you're in the right place at the right time. That "right place" is New York City, where almost all modeling work exists, and the "right time" is whenever your type happens to catch the fancy of an editor, photographer or advertiser. Other necessary ingredients for success: dependability that will get you to assignments on time and in shape, self-reliance to help you through the long and lonely evenings (your social life will be curtailed, partly because you'll meet few young men, partly because your face is your fortune and requires extra hours of sleep to keep it fresh).

Still want to try? Then get experience now modeling for the local department store and in school and club fashion shows. Perfect your makeup technique, experiment with hair styles, work at developing a sure fashion sense. Keep yourself in good physical shape through sound nutritional habits and regular exercise. And save your money! If, after graduation, you still want to follow your star, you'll need enough cash in the bank for a round-trip ticket to New York and expenses for two or three months in a girls' residence club while you try your luck making the rounds of model agencies, photographers, advertisers and magazines. Maybe you'll hit it big (the percentages are against you, but there *are* girls who make $50 to $60 an hour under the lights— and love it!), maybe you'll be disappointed, maybe you'll simply decide that the career of model wife beats that of model. It's your choice!

Q. *I don't know what I want to do when I get out of high school. Maybe I can go to college, but I might have to work*

*right after high-school graduation next June. I've held all
sorts of after-school jobs and I'm pretty good at anything I
turn my hand to. I work hard and learn fast, bosses say. The
only thing I know for sure is that I want to make a good
salary and work steady. What fields offer the best opportunity for a guy like me?*

A. Ask Uncle Sam! The U.S. Government Printing Office
has available a book, *Occupational Outlook Handbook,* with
employment information on major occupations from A (ac-
counting) to W (welding). No word on X-Y-Z jobs.
Evidently xylophone makers, yacht builders and zebra
keepers aren't much in demand. The price for the volume
is $4.50 (separate leaflets on individual occupations included
can be obtained singly for fees ranging from five to fifteen
cents); send check or money order (no stamps) to Superin-
tendent of Documents, Government Printing Office, Wash-
ington 25, D.C. The book will help you match your abilities
to the occupations in which there are the greatest employment opportunities. It would be hard to find a better investment for $4.50.

Q. *Do you think it's possible for a girl to combine marriage and a career and make a true success of both? My
mother keeps saying that a woman should resign her job
when she marries, but that seems to me a complete waste
of a college education. And how's a woman going to go
back to work after her children are grown if she's lost touch
with the business world? I want to get married and I love
children, but I also look forward to an exciting job when I
get out of college two years from now.*

A. When you trade your B.A. for an MRS., you'll need
every bit of learning you picked up in college. Marriage and

motherhood are among the most demanding (and rewarding) jobs a woman can have. You'll find it a challenge to
your knowledge and ingenuity and personal strength to
play the multiple roles of wife, mother, practical nurse, cook,
accountant, dietitian, laundress, child guidance counselor,
clothing expert *and* valuable member of the community.

Staying home with the children during at least their pre-
school years makes the most sense for the majority of
mothers—and children. But some women, because of special
talents or special drives, need to work outside the home
during those years to feel that they're complete human
beings. Then the successful combination of marriage and
career is possible with a co-operative and understanding
husband, an excellent housekeeper-mother substitute—and
the strength of several horses!

Even if you choose to play your mother-wife role to the
hilt, twenty-four hours a day on the home front, you needn't
lose touch completely with the business world. The hand
that rocks the cradle can do lots of other things at home. A
secretary can type manuscripts for writers or term papers
for students, or special reports for local business firms. A
writer can work while the children nap. Artists are able to
free-lance for magazines, newspapers, ad agencies and
department stores. Many arts-and-crafty women make items
(covered wastebaskets, fancy matchbooks, decorative
candles, unique aprons, original design baby clothes,
jewelry) for sale through specialty shops or by mail.

If you keep your earning skills in practice, when it's time
to go back to work you'll have plenty besides "formula
making" and "diaper changing" to list under Experience on
that job application blank!

9 : *Questions* Parents *Ask*

⫿⫿ About Going Steady

Q. *For the first time in her young life, my sixteen-year-old daughter is going steady, and I'm worried sick! Her steady is a nice boy, very dependable and from a good family, but I'm still scared that the intimacy of the relationship will tempt her to go too far. When two normal teenagers see so much of each other night and day, I think they're asking for trouble.*

A. The standards your daughter absorbed from your teaching and example through her first sixteen years are going to be the standards she lives by now, whether or not she goes steady. But it's also true that the constant companionship of going steady can provide additional hazards. It's up to you, her mother, to outline the date rules. Keep her on the same strict date deadline, with penalties if she gets home past the Cinderella hour. (Sometimes couples drift into heavy necking late at night because "there's nothing else to do.") It helps to limit solo dates to once a week, with double dates or crowd activities on other social evenings. Be sure there's always an adult chaperone when

[183

your daughter is entertaining her beau at home. But, above all, make sure she receives all the love and understanding and attention possible from you and her father. Some girls get themselves into trouble because they have a great need to reassure themselves that *"somebody* loves me."

Q. *With my sixteen-and-a-half-year-old daughter and her crowd, going steady is a big thing, and the gossip is driving me out of my mind. They all chatter away like minor league gossip columnists about who's whose, will it last, do you thing he really loves her, and on and on until I want to clap my hands over my ears. I call them the G-Girls (G for Gossip), but they just go on yattering. Is this normal?*

A. Of course, it's normal. But you're not, if you can't cast your mind back to your own high-school days and remember the same giggling gaggle of girls, rehashing everyone's love life. Your daughter and her friends are growing up, and the idea of "belonging" to some special person is new and exciting. They love to talk about their own romances and get a vicarious thrill out of discussing the date lives of their friends. Better take a large dose of patience with your morning coffee; this is going to go on for years. By the way, how come you eavesdrop so much?

Q. *I don't want my sixteen-year-old son to go steady. I'm firmly convinced that sixteen is at least four years too soon to settle on one girl. When I was his age, we played the field, shopped around, looking for* the *girl, instead of pairing off and acting practically like young marrieds. He can't possibly hope to marry and support a family until he's out of college, and that's a long way off. You won't catch me handing out a fat monthly allowance to help support a wife and probably children while he's still trying to get his degree. And every-*

body knows only too well how necessary that degree is these days to get and keep a respectable, well-paying job. I plan to forbid my boy to go steady. What's the best way to lower the boom?

A. Hey, there, you're off on the wrong tack! First of all, for most teen-agers, going steady doesn't mean wedding bells. More often, it's a fairly casual arrangement, meaning "I like you best at the moment" or even "It's convenient to have a date to count on." Most of the couples don't expect the relationship to last very long; very few of them even consider themselves "engaged to be engaged," although they like to go through the motions of acting as if they're in love to last. If you feel strongly that you're son shouldn't go steady in high school, outline your rules and reasons, but don't "lower the boom." Explain why you prefer that he free-lance date, so that you seem a reasonable parent, not a towering tyrant. Above all, don't take the whole thing so seriously. Your son doesn't.

Q. *Up until now, I've never pulled the stern father gambit with any of my children, but I believe this is the time. My seventeen-year-old son is going steady, and the girl couldn't be more wrong for him. She's pretty, all right; even I have to admit that. And she seems reasonably intelligent. But her qualifications stop right there. She comes from a totally different background, socially and economically. I think it would be disastrous if the romance became really serious. I want to break it up. My wife says I'm taking the thing too hard.*

A. The surest way to bring your son and his romance to a boiling point is to play the heavy father bit. You'll put him on the defensive by criticizing his girl, and he may be just rebellious enough to date her more often and more seriously, just to "show you." Best idea is to simmer down, treat the girl as politely and casually as you have your son's past date mates, for as long as the romance lasts. If you don't put the pressure on, it probably won't last very long. High-school going steady doesn't.

About Topic A

Q. *I am a young minister at a large city church. Our youth club has just begun a series of sex education lectures, with the pastor as chief speaker. I have been astounded at the outcry raised by the parents. I wholeheartedly agree that sex education should be given in the home, but I was stunned and discouraged by the lack of knowledge and the misconceptions of our fourteen-to-sixteen-year-old group. If parents fail in their responsibility to their children in this vital area, someone has to fill the gap. Won't you please urge parents not to neglect this important aspect of their children's education, or at least not to raise a fuss when some other authority steps in where they've failed?*

A. Most educators, clergymen and psychiatrists agree that the home is the ideal place for a child to learn about sex, not in one agitated "birds and bees" lecture just before adolescence, but gradually and honestly as he or she grows up. But some parents aren't emotionally or intellectually equipped to do the job. They ought to be delighted when another responsible adult substitutes. Indeed, many experts in the field believe that sex instruction and discussion for adolescents is best handled by an instructor with an impersonal and detached attitude, so the subject is free of the emotional ties and conflicts of the teen-ager with his parents.

Q. *I always considered myself an intelligent and informed mother and it never occurred to me that I might be old-fashioned. But I think I've failed my fourteen-year-old daughter. When she was a little girl, I always answered honestly and completely whatever questions she asked about sex. Sometimes I was embarrassed, but I think I always managed to hide it. What worries me now is that she no longer asks questions, just at a time when I'd think she'd be most curious, since she's becoming seriously interested in boys. What should I do?*

A. Even if you were successful at hiding your embarrassment at her early questions, your teen-aged daughter will still be uncomfortable about reopening a discussion of sex with you. At fourteen, she's probably well-informed on the basic facts, from answers you gave her as she grew up, from discussions with her friends, from reading. But in case any questions remain unanswered in her mind or she has received garbled or conflicting information, it would be a good idea to make available to her a book of sex information written for her age group. With the subject out in the open again, she may come up with questions. But don't be surprised or worried if she doesn't. She has found her own answers.

Q. *My husband isn't speaking to our fifteen-year-old son —at least not about important things. He just won't have a "facts of life" talk with our boy. My husband was brought up in a very strict home where "sex" was considered a dirty word, and he can't bring himself to discuss the subject. I think a young man must face the world armed with knowledge and truth, but I can't convince my husband of this. He says that's what biology classes are for. I believe it should be man to man.*

A. Start by giving your son a book on sex geared for his age. Your clergyman, family doctor or the high-school or local librarian will be helpful with recommendations. Then ask a wise and trusted friend or relative to have the talk your husband balks at. A favorite uncle, an athletic coach, a well-liked family doctor or a clergyman who is good with young people—any of these would be ideal for the job. With an adult other than his parents a teen-ager will feel more free to ask questions on matters that puzzle him and to discuss his own attitudes and worries openly and objectively.

Q. *Our fifteen-year-old son and his friends have a new sport: girl watching! They've found a tall tree not far from the local beach club where, with the help of binoculars, they spy on girls sun bathing.*

A. You can't take away your son's interest in the female form, but you can take away his binoculars. Base your objection on the grounds of manners as well as morals. There's a difference between a healthy interest in the opposite sex and ill-mannered, immature ogling.

Q. *The other day I came unannounced (with an armful of laundry—I usually knock) into my thirteen-year-old daughter's room and found her reading a sex manual for married couples. I have nothing against the book, which is written by a reputable doctor, but I think it's several years too early for her to absorb such detailed and specific information. I'm puzzled at her interest, because I've been very frank with her about the facts of life, starting with answering her very first questions when she was a small girl and continuing to answer her more mature questions as she grew older.*

A. If your daughter isn't reading the book for information, then she's reading it for a vicarious thrill. In early teens, girls have a sudden strong reawakening of interest in sexual matters. Substitute a book of sex information written for teen-agers and tell her you'd much prefer she read the other a few years from now.

About Getting Along with Teens

Q. *I am the mother of three teen-aged children who are on school holiday. I wish they didn't think of vacation from school as vacation from all chores and routine. I have to nag them to tidy up their rooms and get home on time for meals. They think I'm a stickler for schedule and urge me to relax and enjoy our vacation more. What they really mean is to stop nagging them.*

A. Your three children have been following a strict routine through nine months of school, and it's a joy for them to kick up their heels and forget about the clock for a while. Why not let them, without adding a burden of guilt to spoil the fun? Organize life to give them a maximum of freedom and, incidentally, give yourself a respite from household chores. Make it clear they're still responsible for keeping their rooms reasonably neat, but if they want to shut the door on an unmade bed to go off for a sunrise horseback ride—why not? And wouldn't a less rigid meal schedule (cold cuts, deviled eggs and a chilled soup in the refrigerator, everone on his own for supper) make your life easier? The summers when your children will be around are almost over. It would be more fun for everyone if you were a less perfect housekeeper and a more relaxed mother while there's still a chance.

Q. *We never had any trouble raising our two elder girls, but our fifteen-year-old son has become impossible. Not that he is delinquent in any way, but because he is upsetting the whole house with his untidiness, bad manners, tardiness— I could run on all day. His room is a nightmare, he rarely gets to the dinner table on time, is behind in his homework, and a dozen other irritating things. On top of this, he sulks when I talk to him about his habits. Is there any way a boy that age can be taught a sense or responsibility?*

A. Yes, if you're willing to take things two or three at a time and still let him feel he is living to please himself, not just you and the household. Does he have the basic equipment, for example, to help him keep a responsible school schedule? Does he have his own alarm clock, calendar, desk for school work and a bit of privacy for study? Are meals in your house served at a regular hour or is he late by accident? Have you made the rules of the home clear, such as get-home time after parties and movies, time on the telephone, etc.? Fifteen-year-olds are usually dreamy and seemingly unco-operative. But if you insist on co-operation in only a few things, with a minimum of instructions and criticisms, the boy will try. Above all, make an attempt to stay understanding and friendly. Three or four years from now, this "troublemaker" will be off at college or in the army—and think how neat and empty his room will look then.

Q. *My two teen-agers, fourteen and sixteen, are always wailing, "Mother, you just don't understand!" and I'm beginning to agree that they're right. Bone of contention this month: telephone habits. I just can't understand why they find it necessary to phone a friend they've spent all day at school with and talk for half an hour, even when they're going to see each other at school the next day. It's driving me wild.*

A. Your adolescents are going through a tough time in life, meeting new challenges, experiencing new emotions, undergoing physical changes. And all these things happening at once can leave a teen shaken and unsure, without knowing exactly why. Endless chatter with someone the same age who is undergoing the same difficulties can bolster confidence and strengthen egos, even if the conversations seem aimless and unsatisfying to an adult listener. The answer? Decide what you think is a reasonable amount of time for your teens to talk on the phone, within the bounds of family convenience, homework demands and your own strained patience—and then double it. Heckle them as little as possible about chatter time. They aren't hanging on the phone to annoy you, but are seeking a necessary reassurance and sense of belonging. With patience and an enormous amount of good will, you may *all* survive the telephone tangle.

Q. *Our oldest son is seventeen and a wonderful boy. We have two smaller children who still need baby-sitters. My husband and I like to go out and he insists that the seventeen-year-old stand by for sitting service whenever necessary. I feel this is too hard on the boy and that he'll resent it terribly.*

A. If your son just happens to be sitting at home anyway, he's probably glad to stand guard over the young ones. But if your social life is cutting into his, it's time for a family pow-wow: turn and turnabout on baby-sitting. When you know a big date night is coming up for your son, trim your own plans or hire an outside sitter. If *you* have a special evening planned, it is only courtesy and consideration to alert him in advance and *ask* for his help. Most teen-agers don't resent making themselves useful, as long as they're treated as family, not as unpaid help.

Q. *Do all teen-agers go through hysterical phases? Our sixteen-year-old is pretty, has enough dates and gets good grades in school, but she is so emotional that her date life is getting to be too much for us. She has gone to three formal dances recently and each time has left the house in near tears, with her father raging and complaining. At the last minute everything goes wrong. She hates us, hates her dress, hates life in general. Then she comes home to report she had a lovely time! What's the answer.*

A. Your daughter is like an actress with opening night jitters. It's a common teen complaint—too much excitement, too little experience. You might try one of two schedules. Either advise your daughter to give a dress rehearsal the night before a dance, modeling her clothes, her hairdo, etc., making sure all accessories are in order. Or invent a family errand that will take you out of the house until a few minutes before she leaves for the dance. Come home just in time to admire and fluff a ruffle or two. Even great actresses find it hard to put on a scene without an audience.

Q. *I brought my note pad and pen upstairs so I could give you an exact picture of what I'm looking at. What would you do with a sixteen-year-old daughter who leaves her bed unmade, hangs a sweater over a lampshade, a skirt on a door handle and last fall's football banner over a portrait of her grandmother? Week in and week out, her bedroom is like something hit by a whirlwind. She herself is neat as a pin, and pretty. But her bedroom is beyond belief. Any criticism only brings the routine "Oh, Mother!"*

A. Your daughter needs an alarm clock, a schedule and an ultimatum—all provided by you. Few teen-aged girls have the time to keep their headquarters thoroughly buffed up, but they do have time for bed-making and tidying. Weekdays, ten minutes; Saturdays, one hour. Arrange to have your daughter start the day earlier and finish it neater. If she won't co-operate, just close the door on Hurricane Daughter and forget about it. When you *stop* worrying about keeping her bedroom neat, she will *begin!*

Q. *I'm the mother of two teen-aged sons, fourteen and seventeen. We have rented a cottage at a nearby lake for a month this summer and the boys want to invite a friend each for a week's visit. I've spent too many years cleaning up after messy males to really relish the idea. When does Mother get a vacation!*

A. Mother gets a vacation when she makes it clear to the grown males in the house that, although vacation housekeeping chores will be kept to a minimum, they're partly responsible for running things. Let your sons know that their guests are welcome, if—And then lay down the rules: each boy makes his own bed and tidies his own clothes, runs errands when necessary, helps with after-meal clean-up. You might also suggest frequent cookouts, when the males can handle the chef chores. This still leaves the boys with plenty of time for sunning and funning—and gives you a chance to lie in the sun and relax, too.

Q. *Our thirteen-year-old daughter resorts to the sulks when she doesn't get her own way. She goes into a snit over almost anything: not being allowed to buy an expensive or unsuitable dress, not being allowed to date, being asked to neaten her room. I'm so tired of tears and tantrums and bad temper that I'm ready to blow my top myself. What's the answer?*

A. At thirteen, your daughter simply shouldn't be allowed to get away with continual bad behavior. Next time she goes into the sulk routine, send her to her room—and suggest she clean out the drawers and closet while she's there. Invite her back to join the grown-ups when she's ready to behave like one.

Q. *A problem has come up with my fourteen-year-old daughter and I don't know exactly what to do. My husband is a doctor and needs to keep the phone clear for emergency calls. I've always restricted myself to five-minute chats with my friends, but this is too much to expect of a teen-aged girl. She's begging for a phone of her own and I'm tempted to have one installed for her birthday. My husband says this is spoiling her.*

A. It's your husband who needs his own phone, not your daughter. Have one installed, listed under his name, with the second or family phone listed under your name. Then your daughter will have the privilege of reasonable use of the phone and, at the same time, learn self-discipline and sharing.

Q. *My sixteen-year-old son and my husband are at such swords' points these days that life is impossible. They argue constantly; whenever my son voices an opinion on politics or world affairs or even sports, my husband tells him he doesn't know what he's talking about, and they're off. My son is threatening to leave home, and I'm at my wit's end. I love them both. What can I do?*

A. Try to persuade your husband to employ some of the give-and-take tolerance he allows adults who don't share his views. A certain amount of rebellion in a teen-age boy is normal and desirable. He's testing his wings, trying to see how far he can push his parents, striving for independence. A little courtesy and quiet respect for each other's views can turn a "fight" into a stimulating "intellectual discussion." You may have to act as referee for a while, but that's a job at which women are intuitively good.

Q. *On my birthday last week my fifteen-year-old son gave me a bright new lipstick. Last Christmas I found perfume and a new compact in my package from him. Do you think he's trying to tell me something?*

A. Your son is either trying to say that you're a pretty mother and he's just come to realize it *or* that he'd be pleased if you perked up your appearance so he could be more proud of you. An honest look in the mirror will tell you which his message really is.

Q. *My thirteen-year-old daughter is just about impossible to live with. She talks back, she's disobedient, sloppy, lazy— just about every unattractive quality you could mention. She used to be sweet and co-operative, but now I've almost given up on her. I've told her that if she continues to act like a child, I'll treat her as a child, and go back to spanking as punishment. What do you think of spanking as a discipline for adolescents?*

A. Before blaming your daughter completely, better take a look at how you've been handling her lately. Is she being strangled by the silver cord? Are you still trying to run her life completely, instead of allowing her the freedom to make decisions she's capable of making? Are there too many rules to follow? Is she getting the love and appreciation and approval necessary to go through the trying years of early adolescense? Spanking is rarely an effective discipline at any age, but it's particularly unwise in the teens. In trying to calm and control a rambunctious, rebellious teen-ager, seat-of-the-pants intuition works better than seat-of-the-pants punishment.

Q. *The other day I discovered that my daughter and a group of her friends had been playing ghoulish telephone tricks on unsuspecting people. The girls would phone a number picked at random from the book, tell whoever answered that they were calling from the husband's place of business and that there'd been an accident—and then they'd hang up. They always phoned back within a few minutes to say it was a trick, but I'm appalled by their heartlessness and cruelty. I have forbidden my daughter to see any of these girls again. Do you think I was right?*

A. What your daughter and her friends did was unthinkable, of course. But don't make the punishment so severe that her realization of the cruelty of her "joke" is drowned out by her feelings of rebellion. Such telephone pranks are the kind of malicious mischief that young people can get into in a group, without anyone stopping to think clearly. Ask your daughter to ponder the effects of her hoax on the people she called and then talk it over with her in a week, so that she truly understands why she is being punished. Make sure, too, that the other girls' parents know what they were up to. It's important that the girls never play such a trick again, not just because they've been *told* not to, but because they clearly realize how cruel and heartless it is.

Q. *Our fifteen-year-old daughter never asks my advice or opinion anymore. We used to have long, marvelous talks about the world and our place in it, and she'd come running to me with all her problems. Now she's very secretive with me, though she spends hours on the phone with her girl friend and they shut themselves away to talk and giggle endlessly. Every discussion we have, even impersonal ones such as over politics, ends in arguing and tears. What did I do wrong?*

A. Nothing! You're simply describing the typical pattern of adolescence. As children grow, they begin to look beyond their parents for example, information and inspiration. More and more they turn to other adults and to their own contemporaries. Your daughter is experimenting with her new desire for intellectual and emotional independence, testing her beliefs against those of her friends. In short, she's growing up and, inevitably, away from you. If you try to return things to an earlier stage of dependence, when she came to you for advice on everything and you told her not only what you thought but what she should think, it can only mean trouble. In discussions, it will help to *listen* to her opinions, and *volunteer* yours. One of the best ways to get along with a teen-aged girl struggling to gain independence is to give her the respect and attention you'd give any other human being with emotions, drives, opinions and sensibilities of her own. Because that's exactly what she is.

Q. *Last weekend our sixteen-year-old son was brought home by the police at 2 A.M. The officer said he and three other boys had been "loitering" in a residential area. They let him off with a warning that he'd be booked if he was picked up again. Our boy has never been in any trouble and says he and his friends were waiting for another buddy to get home from a date. Why should a youngster be treated like a common criminal?*

A. If your sixteen-year-old hasn't been in trouble yet, he will be soon, wandering around foot-loose at two in the morning. If you don't want the police to enforce the law, set up some rules for your son's behavior and enforce them yourself. Aren't you the least bit curious about where he is and what he's doing on the town in the middle of the night? Give him a sensible deadline and see that he sticks to it—or don't act surprised the next time a policeman appears on the doorstep in the small hours.

Q. *With a daughter graduating from high school this year, my husband and I are confronted with the problem of after-graduation trips. One group of girls has a car trip planned to a large city, going unchaperoned. We have refused our daughter this privilege, feeling she is too young and inexperienced to go off on her own this way. Would you comment on this type of unchaperoned trip? What about conducted tours? What substitute can we offer her so she won't be too disappointed?*

A. High-spirited high-schoolers off on a trip without adult supervision are just asking for trouble—and frequently get it. As a substitute, you might suggest hosteling. If your daughter is an outdoorsy type who makes friends quickly and gets along well with people, hosteling may be the answer for her post-graduation trip. Biking from place to place with a congenial group of fellows and girls her own age, staying overnight in supervised hostels, can be a great way to see the country, learn independence and have a marvelous time. Write American Youth Hostels, 14 West 8th Street, New York 11, New York, for information. Con-

ducted tours planned for teens may also appeal to your
daughter. Ads for these appear along with camp and school
ads in the Sunday newspapers. Ask the tour to refer you to
a recent participant from your area, so that you can reassure
yourself that the program is adequately planned and supervised, and your daughter can find out firsthand whether the
idea really appeals to her.

About Teens and Their Date Life

Q. *The teen-agers in our community begin to date at a
ridiculously early age, and my husband and I strongly disapprove. But our thirteen-year-old daughter wails, "Everybody is doing it!" and it's hard to resist that kind of pressure.
Do you have any hope to hold out to beleaguered parents
like us?*

A. You can be sure that there are plenty of other parents
with just the same complaint in your community. They're
worried, too, about the effects of too-early dating on their
teens' school work and on their ideally paced social develop-
ment. They're concerned about the teen tendency to go
steady with the first boy who asks and the rash of young
marriages. Since there's strength in numbers, why not get
together with other parents and discuss setting up a code of
social behavior for all your blossoming teens? Then when
your daughter wails forlornly, "*Everybody* is doing it," you
can reply with equal vehemence, "Everybody is *not!*"—and
make your rules stick.

Q. *Please help me get myself out of trouble with my
sixteen-year-old daughter. The other day I was cleaning her
room and, thinking I was doing her a favor, I mailed a letter*

to her boy friend which was on her desk. It turned out that they had had a fight and she had written the letter in anger, just to get things off her chest, and never intended mailing it. There was no way for me to know that, and I'm still in the doghouse for fair. What can I do to patch things up?

A. About the only thing you can do is apologize and ask your daughter if she'd like you to try to explain things to the fellow. (She won't accept the offer, but at least you can make it.) When she simmers down and is no longer so embarrassed, she can probably patch things up with the boy. But both you and she can learn something from this incident. At sixteen, your daughter is old enough to mail her own letters—*and* clean her own room!

Q. *For several weeks, my sixteen-year-old daughter has been dating a very attractive boy. The other day she confessed that she doesn't really care for him at all, but enjoys being seen with him because he drives a convertible, is considered a catch and takes her to fancy places. I'm ashamed of her for leading him on this way, but I don't want to interfere. He's such a nice lad that I wouldn't like to see him hurt, especially by my own daughter.*

A. Your daughter has had sixteen years to absorb the principles of fair play, and you can only sit tight and hope that her conscience will catch up with her. Any pressure from you at this point will only put her on the defensive. You might try asking, as calmly as you can manage, "Do you think you're being fair to Steve?" That may be all the prodding her sense of fair play or honesty or kindness needs.

Q. *We have a son, sixteen, who is extremely handsome. This isn't just the fond mother talking. Every girl in his class seems to agree with me. And most of them are on the phone with him sometime during the week. A minimum of three girls phone each night, interrupting our dinner or Mike's homework. He's flattered, of course, by the female attention, but also irritated. He says he'd like to be the one to do the pursuing.*

A. With your son's permission, step into the role of his "social secretary." When a fluttery female voice asks for Mike when he's immersed in homework or TV, say that he can't come to the phone but you'll be glad to take a message. Since it's handsome Mike, not you, they want to talk to, your running telephone interference for him will cut the calls in half. An unlisted phone number is the last resort. But he can't be *that* handsome!

Q. *Please help a doting dad out of trouble. I have only one daughter, a lovely but shy sixteen. Saturday night she was very excited about going to a party and when her date stood her up I blew my top, phoned the boy's father and told him what a cad I thought his son was. When my daughter found out what I'd done (evidently the word was all over school by noon Monday), she burst into tears, told me I was an "interfering parent" and said she'd never forgive me.*

A. At sixteen, your daughter should be allowed the privacy to work out her own difficulties with date mates. By interfering, you made matters much worse. Instead of having a good cry in the haven of her bedroom, she was embarrassed in the eyes of her whole class. You owe her an apology and a promise to maintain a hands-off attitude in the future.

Q. *Our daughter, who is a college junior, became en-gaged to a boy from out of town. He came to visit us, stayed in our home and seems like a good choice. They plan to be married after graduation. My only complaint is his stiffness with me. He seemed awkward in talking to me and almost addressed me as "Hey, you!" to get my attention. Our daughter has always called me "Mother" and I assumed anyone joining the family would do the same thing. Isn't that correct?*

A. No! This boy is not *joining* a family; he is starting one of his own. And since he has a mother of his own, that intimate word may already be used up in his vocabulary. Why not do the warm and welcoming thing and mention to him what name you prefer to be called by—Mother Ann, a favorite nickname, whatever makes both of you most comfortable. Don't let a small thing like this break down communications. Put the boy at ease while he's still talking to you!

Q. *For three months now my sixteen-and-a-half-year-old daughter has been dating a boy from her class. We've known him ever since they entered high school together, but we have never met his parents. We hear they are very nice people, but I feel strange that we have never been intro-duced. The boy practically lives at our house, but even my daughter has met his parents only once. Should I take the initiative and invite them to dinner?*

A. The young twosome might panic if you made a serious effort to get together with the fellow's family. They're just dating; they're not engaged. If either of the teens suggests a meeting, fine. Or if you should meet the boy's parents at a school function, perfect. But don't seek them out deliberately or the young couple (and the other set of parents) will think you're taking the romance much too seriously.

Q. *I have a fifteen-year-old daughter and never had any reason to distrust her until lately. But I have just found out that she lied to me when she came home late from a date the other night. I had been sitting up waiting for over an hour, worried sick, and when she came in I was both relieved and angry, and asked her crossly where she'd been. She stammered and said her date's car had run out of gas. Several days later she admitted they'd gone to a friend's house for an after-movie snack and lost track of time. How can I trust her again?*

A. You don't have too much reason for worry, since your daughter eventually came up with the truth without prodding. Sometimes teens feel backed into a corner by a parent's anger or other pressures and, at that moment, it doesn't seem safe to tell the truth. You can get back on your old footing with your daughter by letting her know you're glad she could admit her fib and assuming that she won't find it necessary to lie again. If you help by listening calmly when she's in trouble, she probably won't.

Q. *I can't help overhearing my seventeen-year-old daughter bragging all the time about the boy she's dating. It's true that he's handsome, does well in school and is a topnotch athlete, too. But I feel she is going to lose friends by constantly talking about how great he is. When I remember my high-school days, I know I never liked girls who were too smug about their conquests.*

A. Your daughter can't help bragging about her guy, partly because she really thinks he's special, partly because it makes her feel special, too, to realize she could land such a prize. Let her savor her conquest, with only a mild word of warning that too much talk will stir up envy among her less lucky friends. Just be careful not to squash that wonderful feeling of "What a lucky girl I am!"

Q. *Do you think there's ever any excuse for opening a daughter's mail or reading her diary? I'm worried about my seventeen-year-old and the boy she's dating. He seems too old and too sophisticated for her, and I'd like to check up on how things are going.*

A. If you want to know how things are going, *ask.* If you're concerned about her seeing so much of the boy, cut down the number of dates she's allowed to have with him. Or insist that, except for one night a week, she double-date. Or move her date deadline to an earlier hour. But stay out of her mail and her diary, which are strictly private property. Intrude with the excuse that you're trying to solve a problem and you'll simply create a bigger one.

Q. *During the Christmas holidays our fifteen-year-old daughter went to visit her cousin in a town fifty miles away and met a seventeen-year-old boy who is very interested in her. Since then he has come to visit her every other weekend, for a total of eight visits. He arrives after dinner on Friday, they go to a movie, then come home and visit with us until midnight. He stays with an uncle in town, arrives after breakfast in the morning and they go off for the day together. They spend the afternoon at art galleries, museums, shopping, etc., come to our house for dinner, then go to a movie or dance or party. Sundays are the same; he comes after breakfast, takes her to church, they spend the afternoon to-*

*gether and he drives back home around dusk. I think this
concentrated togetherness is unwise for our daughter, and
it's limiting our family life. My husband and I have to plan
to be at home during the weekends he visits. My daughter
thinks that, since they see each other only twice a month, the
time together is no more than they'd spend with each other
altogether if he lived in the same town. We want to do the
right thing. He's a nice youngster and devoted to our girl,
but I'm convinced this is too much of a good thing.*

A. This feast-and-famine togetherness is too much like
playing at being engaged. It would be wiser if the boy cut
his visits down to once a month and arrived midday Saturday, instead of Friday night. The constant concentrated
companionship, added to the glamour of having an out-of-
town beau, can be too much emotion for a fifteen-year-old
to handle. You can make your case more strongly with your
daughter if you mention that the fellow is likely to become
bored with her and the too-frequent commuting. It's a point
for your side—and it may even be true!

About Brother and Sister Problems

Q. *I have two daughters, one sixteen, the other fourteen.
The fourteen-year-old is so awful to her older sister that she
is making life in our household unbearable. The older girl
is sweet and gentle and patient, and hardly ever com-
plains, but her sister constantly devils and teases and taunts
her until it all ends in tears. I've tried talking to the younger
girl, scolding her, punishing her, but to no avail. I'm worn
out.*

A. Sounds like a clear-cut case of sibling rivalry, and as
you've already found out, you can't *force* your daughter into

behaving properly. But with love and patience, you can perhaps *persuade* her. She evidently feels that her older sister gets extra love and attention and privileges and that she's low girl on the totem pole. For a month's time, try to skip all criticism and concentrate instead on complimenting her on her good points, praising her for jobs well done, allowing her special privileges (not bribes) when she has deserved an extra treat. Once she feels sure that she's getting her fair share of love and attention, she'll stop demanding it in such unattractive ways.

Q. *We have three teen-aged children—and not a moment's peace and quiet! Our two sons, fourteen and seventeen, and our daughter, fifteen, argue and bicker and scream at each other every waking moment. I don't think I can take it anymore. They don't even seem to* like *each other.*

A. Even if they don't *like* each other, it's your job to insist that they at least are *polite* to each other. Simple good manners can eliminate many brother-sister problems. Undoubtedly there's a great deal of rivalry among teens so close in age, but it can't be allowed to disrupt the household completely. Call a family meeting and outline the new house rules: no arguing (the difference between an "argument" and a "discussion" is often the volume or tone of voice in which it's conducted), no teasing, no clothes borrowing without permission, no invasion of privacy. Then list the penalties for infractions of the rules: cutrailment of TV hours, cuts in allowance, extra household chores, restricted date privileges, whatever would work best with your crew. Make it clear that the code applies to everyone, and don't back down, even though they may sulk and complain for a time. Teen-agers actually welcome rules and standards of

behavior to let them know what's expected of them and
exactly how far they can go. You tell them.

About Teen Personality Problems

Q. *At sixteen, our daughter is a mousy, retiring "intellectual" type who seems to like books rather than boys. To
help her get her date life started, we've been arranging for
her to meet and go out with boys of similar bookish bent.*

But she withdraws even further into her shell on these occasions—and so do the boys. I'd let her work out her problem alone if I didn't sense that she's really miserable about her lack of dates.

A. Why not leave the inside of her head alone for a while and help her work on the outside? Stake your daughter to a professional hair styling, advise her on grooming and cosmetic aids, arrange for her to take ballet or modern dance lessons. Take her shopping for clothes to spice up her wardrobe, subtly steering her away from mousy color and style choices. Help her to become a truly feminine girl, as well as a brain. Once her ego is boosted by her improved appearance and new skills, she'll be better equipped to "work out her problem alone."

Q. *A year ago our son, then fifteen, was a shy, awkward, stringy youngster who didn't excel at anything. He started a "home improvement project" on his own, worked at brightening his personality, became more outgoing, spruced up his personal appearance, began getting better marks, and even made the track team. Suddenly, he has become very boastful, critical (of his friends and of us), superior in his attitude. He's so obnoxious now that I honestly think I preferred him when he was less successful, but more likable.*

A. Give your son a chance to get used to the glories of being good at things at last. By his boasting and display of superiority he's making up to himself for the inner beating he took when he felt left out of everything. He's still trying on his new personality for size. Once he feels comfortable with all the changes he has made, he'll show off less. Try to be patient. Eventually you'll like him again—almost as much as *he* likes *himself* now!

Q. *We have three daughters, the youngest fifteen. Her two older sisters were very popular in high school, but Jane just doesn't seem to hit it off with boys, even though she is prettier than her sisters were. What's worse, she doesn't seem to care. She doesn't go out of her way to make herself appealing to boys, and seems perfectly content just to study and spend time with her girl friends. How can I help her get her social life under-way?*

A. As long as *Jane* isn't brooding about the lack of men in her life, why should *you?* She sounds like a late bloomer, so sit back and relax. Since she is contented with her life, don't make her dissatisfied and uneasy by putting the pressure on her to start dating. She is still young. The worst thing you could do is make her *feel* unpopular by your excessive concern.

Q. *My husband and I are worried about our thirteen-year-old daughter and the influence of one of her friends, a strong-willed fifteen-year-old. Our daughter never makes any decisions without consulting her friend. She even phones her in the evening to find out what to wear to school the next day! The fifteen-year-old is a nice youngster and, fortunately, exerts a good influence, but we worry because Julie never decides anything for herself.*

A. Your daughter, at thirteen, is at an emotional halfway house. She no longer likes to ask advice from her parents on daily decisions, but she doesn't feel sure enough of her own tastes to decide things for herself. Gradually, with more experience, she'll assert her independence from her older friend. Meanwhile, aren't you lucky that the fifteen-year-old is a type your daughter can imitate without real worry? Many mothers aren't so lucky.

Q. *Our fourteen-year-old son is so awkward and ill-at-ease with adults that it's pitiful. When we have guests for dinner, he's all hands and feet. If anyone asks him a direct question, he blushes, stammers and stares at his shoes. At dinner with friends the other night, his entire conversation consisted of three "Yeses," two "Noes" and four "I guess so's." He asks to be allowed to have dinner in his room when we're having company, but I feel he has to learn to get along with the older generation sometime, and it had better be soon. I'm ashamed of his lack of poise.*

A. If your son suffers from social stage fright, why insist he "go on" when you have dinner guests? The more times he fails, the more unsure of himself he'll become. Let him get through this awkward period of his life at his own pace, without maternal pushing and shoving. Have him greet your guests when they arrive (he can manage a handshake and "How do you do?"), then turn him loose for the evening. Let him have dinner at a hamburger joint with a friend or go to a movie. Give him the impression that the night out is a treat, not just a device to get him out of the way. He'll come out of his shell when he's ready, as long as an over-eager mother doesn't try to crack it too soon.

Q. *My thirteen-year-old daughter has emotions like a Yo-yo. One day she's fighting and fussing furiously with her girl friend, and I have to listen to the playback of the argument, including dramatic protestations of "I never want to see her again in my whole life!" Next thing I know, they have their heads together, giggling over some private joke, and the storm is over—until the next time. I don't know what to make of her, and I'm sick of the wails and lamentations when things go wrong.*

A. The mothers of mercurial adolescents are all equipped with two ears. That's so complaints can go in one and out the other. It's a marvelous system for preserving your sanity. Try it.

Q. *Our fourteen-year-old son is so jittery and jumpy that it's driving me wild. He's constantly ruffling his hair, straightening his tie, tugging at his ear or kicking the leg of the chair. He's a nervous wreck—and he's making one out of me, too.*

A. Adolescence is a trying time—for the teen-ager and for his parents. The teen's world is expanding rapidly and explosively, the pressures are on from all sides. He's becoming seriously interested in girls, he's concerned over his rapid growth and bodily changes, he's expected to do well in school, get along well at home, and develop a satisfying social life. And all the time he's trying to find his own place in the world, answering his own inner questions of "Who am I?" and "How do I fit into things?" Tensions build up and are released in many small ways: the bang of a door, wild shouts while watching athletic contests, participation in sports, irritating nervous habits such as you describe. You can help by not calling attention to habits which annoy you, by being as uncritical as possible, by relaxing somewhat the demands you make on him at home, and giving him the quiet and serenity to work out his inner problems. Hard job? Whoever said being a parent was easy?

About Smoking

Q. *My seventeen-year-old son smokes, and since I do, too, I don't (or can't) object. But I'm concerned about his smoking in bed. He likes one last cigarette before he falls asleep at night.*

A. That last cigarette before he falls asleep at night could become his last cigarette, period. Lay down the law, firmly and finally, and make sure it's obeyed: No smoking in bed. He may sizzle at your ultimatum, but that's better than burning.

Q. *Although my husband and I don't smoke ourselves, I don't really mind if our son, now sixteen, decides that he wants to smoke. Now I suspect he's smoking on the sly. I object to his sneaking, not his smoking.*

A. If you sense (or Sen-Sense) that your teen-ager is puffing on the quiet, he's trying to avoid expected parental disapproval. Let him know, casually, that you wouldn't object if he decided to smoke, though taking time to point out the disadvantages and possible dangers. The conversation will clear the air—of everything but cigarette smoke.

Q. *My daughter is only fifteen, but she has recently begun to smoke. I'm quite sure it's experimental and part of growing up, but she has such a baby face that she looks ridiculous. I suppose she feels it gives her poise in awkward social moments (it did me, although I'm sorry now I began to smoke in my teens as I did), but that seems a poor reason to start a messy, expensive habit.*

A. Tell your daughter, in a noncritical fashion, why you think it's a bad idea for her to start smoking. Explain that you're sorry you began so early, and tell her why. Then bolster her self-confidence by helping her, through good grooming, the right clothes and practice in social experiences, to achieve the kind of poise that doesn't go up in smoke!

About Drinking

Q. *We have three children in their early teens. Soon the question of drinking will come up. My wife and I would like them to have a safe and sane attitude toward alcohol. I drink moderately; my wife doesn't drink at all. What's the best advice for parents?*

A. Your children have already absorbed some of your own attitudes toward drinking, merely by living in the same house with you and observing. Both of you sound fairly relaxed about drinking, so they're off to a good start. It is a mistake to banish youngsters from the scene at cocktail hour, even though this is "grown-up time," the first chance of the day for husband and wife to have an unfrenzied private conversation. If the children are told to "go read a book," the cocktail seems forbidden and therefore appealing, an adult privilege to be yearned for.

Tell your children the truth about alcohol, starting by scotching the misconception that it is a stimulant. It's not; it's a powerful depressant. But because it lessens the restraints people normally keep on their behavior, they may seem more relaxed. Point out that normal teens don't need a drink to unwind or have a good time. But don't try to fool them into believing alcohol is "poison." They'll know you're lying and discount anything else you may tell them as parent propaganda.

Point out the problems of teen-aged drinking. It's not that a teen-ager is likely to become a compulsive drinker, but that he'll do unwise and perhaps dangerous things when he has been drinking, things he wouldn't even consider if he'd stuck to ginger ale. He might pick a fight with a good friend; say things he'll be sorry for later; make a pass at a girl he wouldn't even wink at when sober; or clobber everyone by driving after drinking.

Help your teens by suggesting how to get out of drinking gracefully. Usually other members of the group won't press alcohol on a friend, *unless* the person says "No" in such a way that it's a challenge to those drinking. And sometimes it's better for a shy teen of legal age to accept a drink and set it down untouched than to risk a showdown with a tease or bully.

Be particularly firm about drinking while driving. Here it's a matter of strict rules, rather than personal conviction. Don't offer your teen a choice, make it for him: Absolutely no drinking if he's driving.

Q. *I strongly believe that alcohol and gasoline don't mix and have tried to convince my eighteen-year-old son of this. But more than once he has come home with liquor on his breath when he has been driving the family car on dates. My wife is more casual, with a "he's only young once" attitude. I'd like to set down some firm rules about driving and drinking. Do you think I'm too strict?*

A. Drinking and driving don't ever mix, of course. But this is doubly true when young drivers are involved. The average adult should wait an hour before driving if he has had three drinks, two hours if he has had four. But a teen, who reacts more readily to liquor, should wait at least one hour for each drink he has had. Make the rules clear to your son: either wait the necessary time or, better still, don't drive at all after drinking. Let your son know you'll pick him up at a party or finance a taxi, if necessary, rather than have him break this code. As long as he understands the reason for the rule, he'll be more agreeable to it. Warn him ahead of time that breaking the rule means a revocation of car privileges for a specified length of time. Be firm, but not harsh, since some teens would rather risk an accident than face the music with their parents. As for your wife: fill her in on the facts and remind her that, although your son is only young once, you both owe it to him to help him grow old.

About Money

Q. *My seventeen-year-old son, a high-school senior, gets a more than adequate allowance, but he's always in financial trouble. And he expects his father or me to bail him out every time. I think it's about time he was responsible for his own budget, and stopped turning to us like a child. For instance, he has a school prom coming up, and wants to borrow money to rent a dinner jacket and buy the girl an orchid. He bought a hi-fi set two weeks ago and I feel he should have planned ahead for his prom expenses and delayed the purchase of the record machine. What do you think?*

A. Prom time is a rough moment to clamp down suddenly. But your son shouldn't be allowed to go on expecting handouts every time he overextends financially. Why not *loan* him the money for the dance, making it clear that it *is* a loan, to be repaid at a fixed rate from future allowance payments? Then warn him, kindly but firmly, that you've come to his rescue for the last time. Suggest that he bank a portion of his allowance so that he won't be caught short in an emergency again. And make sure you stick to your decision, no matter how urgent his needs or how woebegone his pleadings. Eventually he'll learn, though the learning may be painful for you both!

Q. *Our fifteen-year-old son just bought himself a $30 pair of shoes, because this particular kind of imported shoe is the current fad in his high school. It's true he paid for them with his own earnings, but I'm seeing red anyway. He knows we don't have money to spare and his father never owned a pair of $30 shoes in his life. Do you think I'm being unreasonable?*

A. It's bound to be irritating when a teen blows what might feed a family for a week on one pair of shoes, especially when finances are tight. But it *was* his money, presumably to be spent as he chose. And sometimes, for a teen-ager, being a member of the crowd is worth any price. So point out the extravangance quietly and try to keep your patience. The next fad may be 15-cent Yo-yos!

Q. *I'm a mother of three teens, and I'm tired of the complaints about meager allowances. None of the children do anything to help around the house without constant nagging, but they never need reminding when allowance day comes up. I'm sick of playing maid to three strapping teen-agers. I don't get paid!*

A. Call a family conference, outline the chores each teen is expected to perform, and then issue your ultimatum: work done during the week without reminder or no allowances at week's end. Being broke for a week should break the news to them that you mean business!

Q. *We have an only son, born rather late in our lives, and my husband is very proud of him—so proud that it's damaging to the boy, I think. For high-school graduation, my husband gave the boy a credit card, and set no limit on what he could charge. He's been wining and dining girls three or four nights a week, and the bills are staggering. My husband has a very good income, so he can afford it, but I don't think our son's character can.*

A. A frank talk with your husband may help him to see that giving a boy unlimited resources with no strings attached is like inviting a ten-year-old to eat all the blueberry pie he can hold—it won't be good for him. Try to make your husband understand the wisdom of setting a limit on your son's expenditures, revoking the credit card privilege if he doesn't stay within the budget. By tolerating such irresponsibility, your husband is pushing your son toward trouble. And you can't put lawyers' fees on a credit card!

Q. *My fourteen-year-old son sent away for a supply of shoe polish to sell door-to-door, planning to get rich quick, just as the ad in the back of the magazine promised. I told him I thought it was a bad idea (I'd never heard of the brand), but he went ahead, anyway. He finds the stuff impossible to sell, and he's out twenty-four hard-earned dollars. His dreams of affluence are smashed. I feel sorry for him and would like to give him the $24 just to make him feel better.*

A. Your advice was free and your son didn't take it. You can't bail him out of every difficulty and disappointment from now on. He's learned an important lesson, worth every penny of $24!

Q. *Our eighteen-year-old daughter is earning $50 a week after tax deductions. Her bus fare is $5.50 a week, she sometimes buys her lunch, sometimes makes it and takes it from home. Her father and I feel she should pay room and board, now that she is employed, and would like to know what you think would be a fair amount. She irons her own clothes, takes care of her own room and does the dinner dishes about once a week.*

A. The amount of money a newly independent teen should contribute to the family coffers depends on the over-all state of the budget, and on what she plans to do with her earnings. If your daughter is saving for a worthwhile goal—college fund, investment program, trousseau shopping—then you and your husband may give an approving nod to her stashing away as much as possible after paying only a token amount for room and board. But if family finances are rocky and your daughter's contribution can help pay off back bills, hasten liquidation of a mortgage, provide needed buffing up of the house you all share, then a greater percentage of her income would be welcome. It's something you'll have to work out together in a family conference, coming up with a solution that seems fair to everyone. Better not suggest, however, that she contribute more than half of her after-taxes income, or the incentive to work hard for her very own money will diminish.

About Cars

Q. *I wish you'd pass on my message to teen-aged drivers. My daughter's story may make them think a little. A month ago, coming home too late from a dance, my daughter's date speeded up over the legal limit to get her home on time. He hadn't been drinking and usually he's cautious, but he got careless for a moment and hit a car passing on a curve. My daughter is still laid up, though, thank goodness, she isn't permanently injured. But she will miss the second semester at school, much fun with her friends and, worst of all, the boy, who was uninjured, seems to have forgotten all about her. He doesn't even come to visit her anymore. She's lonely and bitter, and I don't blame her.*

A. This word from a mother may help you make the right decision when you're about to press a heavy foot on the accelerator. If it's a choice between watching the clock and watching the speedometer, risk being late for a date dead-line—but don't make this a habit and an excuse. Start for home in plenty of time to avoid risks or you will be driving under nervous pressure, anyway.

Q. *Our seventeen-year-old son has bought a car with his earnings, something he has looked forward to ever since he was in grade school. But now, suddenly, his father and I are very worried. We know he's a good driver and aren't concerned about his safety on the road. But his behavior when he's parked is what's troubling us. I'd like to forbid him to use the car on dates, but I guess it's too late for that. What can we do?*

A. What can you do? Like every other parent of a son almost a man, you can hope that all the training and love and guidance and standards you gave him during the first seven-teen years of his life will stay with him now. But for him to become a man, you can no longer treat him like a baby.

Q. *Our daughter has been pestering us to give her a car for her high-school graduation. She'll be going away to col-lege, where they're not allowed to keep cars on campus, and I think it would be wasteful to spend so much money for something she could only use in the summertime. It isn't a question of economy. We could afford to give her a car, if we thought it would be the right thing for her.*

A. Explain your reasons for saying "No," and then say it again, firmly and finally. As long as money is no problem, offer her the choice of a car or a summer in Europe as a *college* graduation present, provided she keeps her grades up to a certain level. Bet she chooses the summer in Europe!

About Entertaining

Q. *Help, help! And hurry! Our budget can't stand the strain another minute. My sixteen-year-old daughter has an admirer. He's six foot, four inches, weighs almost two hundred pounds, plays tackle on the football team—and eats dinner with us almost every night! He walks Jill home from school, hangs around listening to records and sniffing the good smells from the kitchen and makes absolutely no move to go home. I'm forced to invite him to join us for dinner, and he hasn't once refused. His mother works and doesn't get home until almost eight o'clock, so the poor boy is hungry. I just can't afford to feed him any longer, but my daughter turns pale whenever I suggest she urge him to go home before dinnertime. She says I'm trying to wreck her romance and that I should be proud that she's hooked the star footballer. Proud I may be, but I'm also going broke!*

A. If your daughter is defenseless, then you'll have to try an end-around play yourself. Next time dinner approaches, say, "I'd like to ask you to join us, but we just don't have enough extra for a guest tonight." Try this technique a few nights in a row, and he'll get your signals. Do invite him, however, on nights when you're having something cheap and filling, just to keep the romance flourishing. Otherwise you may have a reverse problem when your daughter goes on a hunger strike!

Q. *My sixteen-year-old daughter gave a big boy-girl party last week, and pleaded so hard that my husband and*

*I "disappear" for the evening that we went out to a movie.
When we arrived home, almost all the lights in the house
were out, couples were necking madly, one boy had passed
out on the kitchen floor (he'd brought a bottle of liquor),
and the place was a shambles. We campused our daughter
for a month, but she says she couldn't stop the kids from
getting wild. She says she raced aroung, turning on lights
and trying to break up the necking, but without success. Am
I being too harsh with her? Perhaps it wasn't really her fault.*

A. It was partly your daughter's fault, mostly yours. Even
if she didn't know better, *you* should have realized it was
unwise to leave a teen party unchaperoned. It isn't necessary
for adults to hover constantly or do sentry duty in the living
room, but your presence somewhere in the house acts as a
deterrent to wild behavior. Next time your daughter entertains, stay at home, unobtrusively if necessary. But *be
there.* You might also suggest she try a different guest list.
This crowd sounds pretty wild to start with.

Q. *I've always tried to make my sixteen-year-old daughter's friends welcome in our home. But they don't seem to
have any respect for the property of others. They flop into
furniture, sit with their feet on the coffee table and leave a
terrible mess of cigarette butts, empty soft drink bottles,
and records strewn all over the living room. I work hard to
make my home attractive for my husband to come home to
at night, but usually all he sees is a teen-created shambles.*

A. Your daughter has to learn, and quickly, that part of
being a good hostess is learning to keep her guests under
control. Calmly discuss house rules with her (respect for
furnishings, clean-up detail when the guests leave, an off-
limits sign on the refrigerator unless refreshments are

offered) and then tell her you expect her to enforce them. Your home should be a place for your daughter and her friends to relax, but not fall apart completely.

Q. *Do you think it's a good idea to let a fourteen-year-old girl spend the night with her girl friend? Ours has always been a closely knit family and I have encouraged my daughter to have her friends here to visit her and to spend the night. But I'm reluctant to let her spend the night away from home herself. Recently she has been begging for permission to visit her best girl friend. We don't know the girl's parents, and I worry about exposing my daughter to a family I know nothing about.*

A. It's marvelous that you have a close-knit family and encourage your daughter to entertain at home. But at fifteen, she must also be allowed to venture out into the world and learn about other families. If it will ease your mind, invite her girl friend's parents to dinner, so that you won't feel she's going to visit total strangers. And then by all means let her spend the night. Give her the greatest gift of all: the chance to begin to live her own life with no strings, apron or otherwise, attached.

Q. *My daughter and I have argued about this so long, we decided to abide by whatever you say. She is seventeen years old, and is constantly pestering to have a pajama party. We have a small house, limited budget and the whole thing strikes me as a lot of nonsense, anyway. Is a pajama party "the most popular form of teen-age party" as she says, or am I right in saying I prefer the old-fashioned kind where girls go home to their own beds?*

A. You're still head of the house, in the housekeeping department, at least. If you feel that such a party is too much trouble and too expensive, take a firm stand and close the subject. *But* teen-agers do like pajama parties, because it means that rare chance of letting the fun wear itself out instead of cutting it short by the clock. Perhaps you'd be wise to relent just once and allow a *small* pajama party. After a hard night sleeping on the floor, your daughter may buy your idea that this is really "a lot of nonsense." But she'll have had fun finding out for herself.

Q. *For her sixteenth birthday, my husband and I re-decorated our daughter's room as a bed-sitting room. It has a couch with throw pillows instead of a bed, a desk, comfortable chairs, her phonograph, etc. It is her retreat from the world and her place to entertain. My husband says it isn't proper for her to entertain her date there, because, even though it doesn't look like it, the room is her bedroom. Since the room is on the first floor, very near our living room, I don't think there is any impropriety. What is your opinion?*

A. You're right. Your daughter's bedroom has become a second living room, and there's no reason why she shouldn't entertain her friends, both male and female, in it. There should always be an adult nearby to act as chaperone, of course, but this same rule would apply whether she had guests in the living room, a basement rumpus room or gathered around the backyard barbecue. In today's era of smaller houses, a bed-sitting room provides a chance for both privacy and propriety for teen-aged hostesses.

Q. *I have a fifteen-year-old daughter who overnight turned from an ugly duckling into a real beauty. Consequently, the house is constantly swarming with gangling males with enormous appetites. They're all over the place, and my husband and I are tired of the lack of privacy. Also,*

I find the food budget is taking a beating. My daughter is forever making sandwiches and cookies and cake for these young men with insatiable appetites. How can we regain our own home?

A. How could you tell that your ugly duckling was going to blossom into an attraction that would require traffic control? Time now to clear the air by setting up new house rules to cover the situation. First rule better be "everybody out by the time Daddy comes home," except for those fellows who are specifically invited for an evening or a meal. Another essential rule is "everybody stays out of the refrigerator." Make it clear to your daughter that the boys must fill up on inexpensive popcorn, pretzels, potato chips and soft drinks, but the cold roast beef is for her father, still the most important male in the house. Then just sit back and try to be patient. Before long, your daughter will narrow her choice of males down to a few, or even just one. Then both your blood pressure and food budget will go down.

Q. *When a teen-aged girl gives a party, who should be responsible for preparing and serving the refreshments, the girl or her mother? Our high-school junior is giving lots of get-togethers, ranging from casual Coke-and-potato-chip record gatherings to more elaborate buffet suppers. I want to help, without intruding, but I also want her to learn to be a good hostess in every way.*

A. It doesn't require much effort on the part of a junior grade hostess to fill bowls with popcorn and potato chips, and to make sure the Cokes are iced and the records stacked on the turntable. But for fancier fare, Mother will have to remain in charge in the kitchen. Your daughter can set the table under your watchful eye and help with whatever food preparation she's capable of. (She'll learn as she watches you.) But it's up to you to see that the baked ham and hot rolls come out of the oven at the right time, that the fudge sauce is hot and the ice cream is cold when dessert time rolls round. For simple parties, let your daughter be completely responsible for clean-up chores, but lend a hand for policing the area after a big blowout. Nothing takes the glow off the memory of a good party like facing a sink full of dishes alone late at night. And you'll find that lots of confidences get exchanged over the soapy suds.

Q. *Last Saturday night our seventeen-year-old daughter, a senior in a good private girls' school, gave her first boy-girl party in more than two years. And it turned out to be a shambles! It was what she calls a "spread the word" party, with no real guest list. She told some of her friends she was having a party and asked them to pass on the word. The boys brought bottles of whiskey, drove their cars over our newly seeded lawn, tore the dining room door off its hinges and, crowning insult, scrawled obscenities on the bathroom mirror with lipstick. When my husband and I returned from the movies at ten-thirty, we were appalled at what we found, and our daughter was just as shocked as we were. How can a party of supposedly "nice" teen-agers get so completely out of hand?*

A. The party began to get out of hand before the first guest arrived. Anything so casual in concept and organization as a "spread the word" party, with its unlimited guest list, automatically lends an air of "anything goes." And the second big mistake was leaving the party unchaperoned. You and your husband should have been there all evening long, even if over the wailed protests of your daughter. It wouldn't have been necessary to police the premises (even though it sounds as if a policeman or two might have been useful in controlling this wild crowd); your very presence in the house would have kept the lid on boisterous behavior. A definite guest list and on-the-scene adults are as necessary ingredients as potato chips and soft drinks for a successful teen-aged party.

About the Way Teens Look

Q. *Our sixteen-year-old son plays on the high-school football team, and at a party the night they won their first game of the season he bleached an orange streak in the middle of his black hair, so his head displays orange and black, the school colors. His father and I are appalled, because he says he's going to keep his hair this way as long as the team continues to win. What can we do?*

A. You can relax and let your son enjoy some of the nutty, exuberant fun of being sixteen. If he feels his lucky streak and the team's lucky streak go together, why fuss? His hair will grow out and he'll grow up.

Q. *My daughter has a very bad complexion problem and seems generally rundown. But whenever I suggest that she go to see our family doctor or make an appointment for her, she balks. I'm worried about her, because I know she's self-conscious about her skin and withdraws from friends because of it. What can I do?*

A. Make an appointment yourself with the family doctor, and ask him if there's a physician in your town who specializes in treating young people. Adolescents often need a personal physician and a doctor-patient relationship which excludes the rest of the family. Give your daughter the name and telephone number of the recommended doctor and suggest that she herself phone for an appointment. Then don't press the matter. Bet within two weeks she has arranged for her own checkup.

Q. *My fifteen-year-old daughter has been told by several different people that she looks like a certain young movie star. The flattery has gone to her head and now she tries to dress like the girl, talk like her and even walk like her. I keep telling her that she'd be much more appealing if she'd only act like her own sweet self, but she just shrugs me off. People in our small town are beginning to notice that she's behaving oddly, and think she is stuck up. I don't know what to do.*

A. All teens go through a period of imitating an admired person. Some girls try to pattern themselves after a favorite teacher or relative or leading member of the crowd. It's all a part of searching for an identity of their own. Your daughter may be overdoing things a bit, her ego having been boosted by being compared to someone successful and famous. You'll just have to ride out this period in her life. Before long, she'll discover on her own that it's more fun and rewarding to be herself. Until that discovery, let her dream a little.

Q. *My husband and I have just moved to the suburbs with our three children, the oldest a boy of thirteen. In the city, there was very little opportunity for athletics, especially since the school the children attended had no adequate sports program. Now we find we are in a very sports-minded community and our son's lack of athletic ability is making it difficult for him to fit in. He's miserable and withdrawing into books and music. I'm afraid he'll never have really close friends here. He's fairly well co-ordinated, but won't go out for sports because he feels so far behind the other boys.*

A. On his own, your son can't catch up with boys who have been playing touch football and sandlot baseball in vacant lots almost since kindergarten. Stretch the budget, if possible, to finance lessons in at least one sport, a sport like tennis or swimming in which he can practice on his own, without having to drum up a whole team and do his learning in front of an audience. Once he begins to realize that he isn't all thumbs and gains a degree of self-confidence that comes from being competent in one sport, he'll be more ready for team games. The ability to play at least one game well will be an asset, both physically and socially, for the rest of his life.

Q. *My husband is a very stern man and, I think, overly strict with our sixteen-year-old daughter. He doesn't allow her to date (although mixed parties and dances meet with his approval) and he has expressed the wish that she not wear lipstick. I think this is very hard on the girl. I know that she wears lipstick when she is away from home and wipes it off before her father sees her. I don't approve of her disobedience, but I understand her reasons. Do you think I should speak to her or go on pretending I just don't notice? I feel I should uphold my husband's authority, yet I believe he is excessively strict.*

A. It's often a mother's role to act as buffer and go-between, trying to bring agreement between father and teen-aged children. Begin by trying to convince your husband that he is unnecessarily strict. Try to make him understand that your daughter will feel like an oddball being the paleface among the rest of the girls, and promise that you will oversee her use of makeup so it will be tasteful. But until you convince him, it may be a kindness to your daughter to continue to ignore her minor infraction of the no-makeup rule.

Q. *My fifteen-year-old daughter is slightly overweight (about ten pounds) and her own diet solution to this problem is to skip breakfast. I know this is terrible for a youngster her age, because she hasn't the energy to put the most into her schoolwork, and then she fills up on starchy foods at the school cafeteria at noon. She says she just doesn't have time for a decent breakfast in the morning. How can I convince her she's ruining her health as well as her figure?*

A. Try advancing her alarm clock fifteen minutes and see to it that a decent breakfast is on the table a quarter of an hour before she has to leave for school. If this doesn't work and her excuse is still lack of time, insist that she at least drink an eggnog before plunging out into the world. A skim milk eggnog, artifically sweetened and flavored with vanilla or instant coffee, well beaten, foamy and icy cold, has teen-age appeal, and enough food value to give her a fairly decent start on the day—all in thirty seconds.

Q. *We have two teen-agers, a boy fourteen and a girl sixteen, and their clothes taste makes my hair stand on end. My son wears loud sport shirts and tight black pants, just like all the other boys in his crowd. And my daughter and her friends wear clothes so alike that they look as if they're in uniform. Each child has a clothes allowance (we're trying to teach them to budget and save), but I can't help com-*

plaining about the way they spend it. They don't seem to care about their father's opinion or mine, but are only concerned about whether their friends approve of their clothes. I find it hard to keep my temper and sense of humor.

A. Partly your teens are rebelling against adult tastes and domination. But more importantly, in their rapidly expanding world, they have a need to belong to the crowd and to assume its protective coloration by wearing similar clothes. It's inevitable that you are resentful when their clothes offend your taste and when your children turn to their contemporaries for approval and advice, rather than to you. And it's an added blow to your pride to realize that observers may assume that *their* taste reflects *yours*. But a freedom to make choices, decisions and frequent mistakes is an essential part of growing up and maturing. No amount of criticizing or carping is going to make your teens less eager to be part of the crowd, practically indistinguishable from the others. Their need to play fashion follow-the-leader will pass, and their clothes taste will gradually improve. Meantime, best idea is to keep your eyes—and your mouth!—closed to their more bizarre costumes.

Q. *Our son, fifteen, is awkward and badly co-ordinated and his posture is terrible. I've suggested, as tactfully as possible, that he take up body building or go out for sports to achieve some muscle control, but these suggestions make him angry and moody. He seems unhappy about his lack of athletic ability, so you'd think he'd appreciate some constructive suggestions from his dad.*

A. Adolescence is a time of rapid but uneven physical growth. Often teens slouch because their muscles are simply not capable of maintaining good posture. Feet and hands temporarily too big for the rest of the body and poor muscle control make a boy awkward and uncomfortable with his body. Your son is very aware of his lack of physical skills. Every day he compares himself with friends who are co-ordinated better and with adults who use their bodies skillfully. Self-improvement hints from adults who have passed through this stage of physical awkwardness and have forgotten the unpleasant emotions only remind an adolescent of his shortcomings, of which he's already too painfully aware. He's likely to react with anger, sulkiness or withdrawal. The best solution is to leave your son alone, bite your tongue when you're tempted to give body-building hints, and wait as patiently as possible for him and his body to grow up together.

About Etiquette

Q. *I'm a man of sixty-eight with fairly firm opinions, I know. When I was young, boys were taught to shake hands firmly and look a person straight in the eye when introduced. The boys who come to pick up my fifteen-year-old grand-daughter have the most wishy-washy handshakes I've felt in all my sixty-eight years. I just can't trust them, somehow. Don't parents teach their boys to be men, anymore?*

A. A good, firm handshake is more a test of muscle power than character. Don't be so hard on the young fellows or you'll scare them off. Then you won't be able to look your granddaughter straight in the eye!

Q. *I suppose to teen-agers, half my age, I'll be considered an old fogy. Actually, I'm a bouncy, attractive woman of thirty-two, with a complaint. I'm tired of going to the movies with my husband on the few free nights I have off from my children, and putting up with bad behavior from the high-school crowd. They're noisy, rude and thoughtless, and act as if the movie were being shown just for them. It takes planning and careful budgeting for us to afford a night out, and to have it ruined by popcorn crunched in our ear, heavy-hoofed young men tramping over our feet and ardent love-making by couples who didn't come to see the movie drives us mad. Please pass the word along to teen-agers, who are nice kids at heart.*

A. Teen-agers are sometimes exuberant and thoughtless in their pursuit of fun. But if you keep running into movie menaces, try looking back sixteen years yourself. Sometimes a long memory helps overcome a slightly short temper!

Q. I have a son, fifteen, who brings many of his friends home for after-school snacks. I'm getting tired of discourteous oafs who never bother to rise when a woman comes into the room. They act as if I were a piece of furniture. I'm tempted to give them a lecture on manners, but I'm sure that would infuriate my son.

A. A lecture on manners may be in order—to your son, and in private. If *he* were trained to leap to his feet when a woman comes into the room (yes, even his mother), the other fellows might follow his example. It sounds as if your real grievance is against your son rather than his "oafish" friends. Another point: maybe you're zipping in and out of the room too frequently, mostly to test their manners. The boys have come to visit and relax; don't make them jump up and down as if they were doing calisthenics just because you're in the mood for a big helping of respect.

Q. I feel I must let off steam to someone and, since my sixteen-year-old daughter would just think I was an old-

*fashioned bore, I'm writing you. I try hard to be a good
mother and welcome my daughter's friends to her home.
But I'm tired of being treated like hired help by these
youngsters. I provide the refreshments, clean up after the
parties and am on hand for advice when asked. But in the
past six months, not one teen-aged visitor has said, "Thank
you, Mrs. Little." Is a little courtesy or gratitude too much
to expect?*

A. Better take off that invisible "Kick Me" sign. Let your
daughter know that her friends are welcome but *she's* the
hostess—and it's time she began acting like one. It's up to her
to make the refreshments and neaten up the place after-
wards. Stop *acting* like the hired help, and the teens will
stop *treating* you that way.

Q. *How can I get my thirteen-year-old son to write thank-
you notes? He received many fine gifts for his birthday from
out-of-town relatives, but he just won't sit down to put his
gratitude on paper. I don't want to keep pressuring him, but
I think it's essential that he be polite.*

A. The habit of writing thank-you notes promptly is one
your son should have acquired when he was six or seven,
and copied a brief printed note that you wrote from his
dictation. It's a bit much to expect him to be overtaken by
a sudden passion for politeness at this stage. But it isn't too
late to start. Explain that people went to big trouble and
expense to remember his birthday and it's up to him to go
to the small trouble of thanking them. Bolster your argument
by appealing to his self-interest: no thank-you notes this
year, perhaps no present next year. And cut off TV privileges
until the letters are written. That should do it!

About Date Planning

Q. *I've never believed in urging youngsters to pair off prematurely, but my daughter's eighth-grade class is having a school dance and everyone is supposed to have a partner for the occasion. I think this is rushing thirteen- and fourteen-year-olds into a social situation they aren't ready to cope with. And it causes unnecessary hurt feelings for the girls who inevitably will be left out. (Not my daughter, incidentally, who is pretty and popular with both boys and girls.) I'd like to register a protest, but I don't want to be an old fogy.*

A. Check with some of the other mothers, who very likely feel as you do. If enough of you suggest that the party be simply a group festivity, with no two-by-two pairing off, it's likely the school will change the plans. It's foolish to rush matching partners, when in two years parents and teachers alike will be concerned about the large number of students going steady.

Q. *Our daughter leads a very disorganized date life. I think a mother should know where her child is going and with whom she's going. But whenever I ask her, she says, "Oh, Mo-o-other, we're just going to fool around. I don't know where we'll be." I don't like to nag, but I feel obligated to keep tabs on her. She's only sixteen.*

A. Like the goony bird, your daughter may not know where she's going, but she *does* know where she's been. If her date plans are so indefinite that she doesn't know where she and her fellow friend are going to spend the evening, have her fill you in on the details the next day. Knowing she must report to headquarters, she'll be quite careful to stick to the

date rules you've set up for her. Just be sure she knows
ahead of time exactly what activities you approve of and
what places are off limits for date fun. Don't let her plead
ignorance of the family laws. That's no excuse, and she
knows it.

About School

Q. *I am a guidance counselor at a high school in a well-to-
do suburb of a large city, and the parent of two teen-agers.
I am very concerned about the pressure being put on our
students by their parents to achieve high grades, for the
sake of the grades alone. The emphasis is off intellectual
enrichment and on marks: as a necessity for college entrance,
as "status" (you'd be surprised how many parents get
vicarious satisfaction from their children's school success),
and as yet another way of keeping up with (and beating)
the Joneses. Cheating is on the increase in our school and so
is what the students call "academic payola": rewards offered
by parents for maintaining a certain scholastic level. In our
suburb, straight A's are often worth a Thunderbird and a B
average is enough to get a boy a $10 weekly allowance!
Somebody had better wise up these parents. Their children
are becoming fact-filled machines. Press the right button
(with a multiple-choice test, for instance) and information
spews forth. But they haven't learned to think! And it's
not the kids' fault.*

A. How about more parent-teacher association at the
PTA? One great thing about ambitious parents who want
the best for their children: if they're alerted to what they're
doing wrong and offered suggested solutions, they try hard
to set things straight. But first you have to tell them. When's
the next PTA meeting?

Q. *My son is fourteen and a high-school freshman in a good private school. He is excellent in art and music, the subjects which interest him most, but doing quite poorly in his academic subjects. Whenever we try to encourage him to study more, he says he wants to be an artist, and book learning isn't too important to him. His father and I are frantic. What can we do?*

A. Humans always do best what they like best. And if your son's talent and enthusiasm lies along creative lines, of course that's where he'll excel. Don't downgrade or de-emphasize his achievements in artistic areas; the world needs creative people as desperately as it does scientists and mathematicians. You can only discourage him with compliments that go, "That's a marvelous painting, but how about your math?" You might have his art teacher drop hints that really good artists are generally broad and knowledgeable men. You can provide him with art books and biographies of artists and musicians. Try to interest him in excellence in all things, but don't push him. He's probably getting so much personal satisfaction out of the things he's good at that he doesn't feel compelled to work hard at his academic subjects. Be glad he excels in at least two areas of interest.

Q. *I'd like to register a strong protest against teachers who interfere too much in their students' affairs. My daughter is fourteen, a lovely-looking child with long, graceful legs and a beautiful, slim body. Yesterday her gym teacher phoned me to check on the girl's diet, because the teacher deems her "far too skinny." I couldn't help being annoyed. Our daughter is not underweight and, according to her doctor, is in perfect health (she hasn't missed a day of school in over two years). What irritated me most, I guess, is that I happen to know the gym teacher is a hulking woman, at least twenty pounds overweight, who would benefit by watching her own diet and doing more of her own exercises. How should I have handled the situation?*

A. The best reaction to the phone call would have been a polite "Thank you" to the teacher for her interest and an explanation that your daughter's doctor finds her in excellent physical shape. Some parents are too busy or too indifferent to keep close tabs on teen-agers' health and diet. In trying to alert these mothers, a teacher is bound to step on the toes of conscientious folk like you. The woman was doing her job. Part of your job is to keep your temper in irritating situations.

Q. *My fourteen-year-old son, with a much better than average IQ, shows signs of flunking many of his freshman-year courses. The problem is that he just won't do his homework. His father and I have tried threats and punishment, but to no avail. I wouldn't mind so much if he didn't have a good brain, but this frittering away of talent really bothers me. Any helpful suggestions?*

A. Sounds as if your son is resisting parental pressure as much as book learning. At fourteen, a boy is inclined to dig in his heels when he thinks his parents are trying to run his life. Try putting him on his own regarding homework. Explain to him, once more and calmly, that he'll have trouble getting into college or landing a job of his choice if he doesn't keep up his grades. Then suggest that he set aside a certain time each night for homework, and tell him it's his responsibility for the rest of the semester. After that, don't even ask him about his work. See that he has a quiet place to study, with all the necessary equipment and reference works, but leave him alone. You may be marvelously sur-

prised at how he pulls his grades up when he isn't being
pushed.

About Jobs

Q. *Our daughter, fifteen, wants to increase her baby-
sitting activities and a friend suggested she hang a sign in
the neighborhood laundromat, saying that she's available for
sitting, and giving her rates and telephone number. I don't
feel right about having her go into strange homes, but Jane
says lots of her classmates get jobs this way.*

A. Have your daughter limit her sitting service to friends
of the family and neighbors you know. By accepting any
casual job offer your daughter would be running a risk,
however small, of getting herself into home situations she
might not be able to handle at fifteen. Until she's older and
more experienced, let her accept only "safe" jobs. It wouldn't
be a bad idea if parents wanting to hire baby-sitters were
asked to come up with references. Why not?

Q. *Our sixteen-year-old boy went to work in a neighborhood drugstore after school and over the weekends. I'm
annoyed because he's being asked to do all sorts of dirty
work. He was hired to "help out," and has ended up sweep-
ing the floor, stacking boxes in the dusty stockroom, cleaning
up the fountain, all the messy menial work the owner won't
do for himself. I think he's being taken advantage of because he's young and would like him to quit, but he says the
money is good and the work isn't too bad.*

A. Sounds as if your son has a more realistic viewpoint
than you do. Did you really expect the owner to do the
drudgery and let your son stand around, smiling pleasantly

and doling out aspirin? What you're wishing for is your son to be Instant Boss—and that job's already filled.

Q. *Our son, fifteen, has announced that, instead of going to camp this summer, he wants to get a job. He plans to put his earnings aside to buy a car when he's old enough to get his license. He's asked for our help in trying to locate work, but his father thinks he should be on his own, both in landing and keeping a job.*

A. If your husband is reluctant to ask friends to give your son a summer job, that's understandable. Requesting that someone you know find an opening for a teen can put a strain on a friendship and makes the teen wonder if he could have landed the job on his own. But even if you can't be an on-the-spot employment agency, at least be a steering committee of two. Teens with no job experience, except perhaps mowing neighbors' lawns or washing cars for money, often don't know how to go about finding vacancies or applying for a job. Suggest first that your son outline the kinds of work he *could* do—and *would like* to do. Have him check with the placement service at school: often local businessmen look for dependable help through the school. Failing there, he can check around the neighborhood businesses: does the supermarket need a stock boy or grocery sacker, does the drugstore want a delivery boy or soda jerk, could he be a pump jockey at the gas station around the corner? A prime source of information is, of course, the Help Wanted section of the newspaper.

Be ready with helpful hints when it comes to applying for the job: what to wear, what to say, how to act. And does he have all the necessary papers before he goes job hunting? Does he need a work permit? Social security number?

Letters of reference? This is his first venture into the cold, hard world of business. He deserves all the help you can give him because, though he's the last person who'd ever admit it, he's probably nervous and a bit scared. Once he gets the job, he's on his own. It's up to him to keep it.

Q. *Our seventeen-year-old daughter baby-sits for extra spending money and now our fifteen-year-old son wants to get after-school and Saturday work in a grocery store because he feels like a poor relation. I don't mind Debby's sitting three or four nights a week, because, after the children are put to bed, she can study on the job. But I'm afraid Jeff will run into trouble with his studies if he tries to handle both work and school.*

A. But just try to make Jeff see your point! You probably can't, without putting the project to a practical test. Tell him you're agreeable to his getting a job, if he can hold it without letting his marks fall. The day of reckoning is the first time report cards come out. If his grades haven't suffered, then the job is a plus, giving him income and independence. But if his marks have nose-dived, insist he give up the job or work only on Saturdays. And then you might consider jacking up his allowance slightly, so he won't feel so down at the mouth and down at the heels.

INDEX

Because of the very full Contents for this book, it was decided that this would serve as an Index, rather than repeat the same information here. See pages ix and x.

SHEILA JOHN DALY

columnist for the *Chicago Tribune,* has been a specialist in teenage problems since she was a sixteen-year-old high school senior and began writing a column for teens for the *Chicago Tribune* and syndicate papers.

Sheila John sold her first short story, *The Sisters,* to *Woman's Day* the summer she was eleven. Since then, she has done fiction and feature articles for *Ladies' Home Journal, Saturday Evening Post, Mademoiselle, Seventeen* and a number of other magazines, as well as newspapers. With her three sisters, Maureen (author of the perennial best-seller, SEVENTEENTH SUMMER), Kay (advertising executive) and Maggie (author, fashion authority and columnist), she wrote a monthly feature, *What Are People Really Like?,* for *Ladies' Home Journal.*

Sheila John's first book, PERSONALITY PLUS! appeared when she was a freshman in college. Since then she has written four other books: PARTY FUN, suggestions for teen-age entertaining; PRETTY, PLEASE, a grooming book for high-school girls; BLONDES PREFER GENTLEMEN, an etiquette and date-advice book for teen-aged boys; and QUESTIONS TEEN-AGERS ASK, an edited collection of her answers to questions high-schoolers all over the nation have asked via her newspaper column.

Sheila Daly now lives in New York City with her advertising executive husband and three young sons.

DATE DUE